OVERCOMING OBAMACARE

Three Approaches to Reversing the Government Takeover of Health Care

by Philip Klein

Table of Contents

REPEAL IS NOT ENOUGH 5

THE GOVERNMENT TAKEOVER 15

HAVING HEALTH CARE YOUR WAY 23

THE REFORM SCHOOL 39

THE REPLACE SCHOOL 61

THE RESTART SCHOOL 83

OVERCOMING OBAMACARE 105

Acknowledgments 109

About the Author 111

Chapter 1
REPEAL IS NOT ENOUGH

Ever since President Obama signed his overhaul of the U.S. health care system into law on March 23, 2010, the elusive goal of repealing the legislation has been the driving force behind Republican politics.

Supporting a full repeal of the health care law has been a required position for any Republican seeking federal office since the law was passed, and opposition to the law was at the center of a 2013 budget dispute that resulted in a government shutdown.

American voters have rewarded Republicans for their anti-Obamacare stance. When the first versions of the law passed through Congress, Democrats controlled 59 percent of the seats in the House of Representatives[1] and 60 percent of the seats in the U.S. Senate.[2] By the time the dust had settled on the 2014 midterm elections, Republicans had gained control of both chambers of Congress.

With Republicans now in charge of the Senate and feeling more confident about their chances of taking back the White

---

1   "Affordable Health Care for America Act: Roll Vote No. 887." (Nov. 7, 2009) http://clerk.house.gov/evs/2009/roll887.xml

2   "Patient Protection and Affordable Care Act: Roll Call Vote No. 396." (Dec. 24, 2009) https://www.senate.gov/legislative/LIS/roll_call_lists/roll_call_vote_cfm.cfm?congress=111&session=1&vote=00396

House in 2016, there has been a renewed zeal for repealing the unpopular law.

But repeal is not enough.

If opponents of the law want to win the war over the future of the nation's medical system, they will have to unite around an alternative approach. In the chapters that follow, I explore a number of alternatives to Obamacare, and sort them into three different schools of thought. My process is guided by the belief that one cannot understand policy without appreciating the philosophy that is driving it.

Due to their long-standing suspicions of elected Republicans, many limited government advocates wince at any suggestion of an "alternative" to Obamacare. When Republicans utter phrases such as "repeal and replace," what conservatives often hear is "Obamacare Lite." As a result, the prevailing question on the right often becomes, "Why can't we just repeal the law and be done with the health care issue?"

The answer is that even if simple repeal were politically obtainable, Americans would still be left with a broken health care system. Government regulations would still be stifling competition and individual choice, and as a result, health care would still be too costly. Spending on government health care programs would still be driving the nation's unsustainable long-term debt problem.

If Republicans achieve repeal but do not agree on a way to reform health care along free market lines, it's inevitable that Democrats will eventually lead another overhaul of the system that would grant even more power to the federal government than Obamacare does.

Getting Republicans to unify around a health care strategy, however, is a challenge. Health care policy has traditionally only been a motivating issue for conservative activists when it comes to opposing liberal attempts to expand the role of government. Health care was a hot issue on the right when President Clinton assigned First Lady Hillary Clinton to lead an overhaul of the health care system in 1993. Conservatives led a furious backlash against the proposal, which not only went down in flames, but helped drive the 1994 Republican takeover of Congress.

Once the Clinton proposal was dead, however, Republicans and conservatives went back to largely ignoring the issue instead of developing an alternative health care agenda based on market-oriented principles. That isn't to say that there weren't any people on the right interested in addressing the challenge. Quite the contrary, there were a number of think tanks and policy experts pushing reforms. But such academic debates never translated to any sort of mass appeal on the right.

If you were speaking to a conservative audience during the 2000s and you wanted to fire up the crowd, you spoke about

tax cuts, judges, gun rights, immigration, the War on Ter-
ror, or a number of other issues. But you wouldn't anticipate
raucous applause if you had shouted, "And then we have to
equalize the tax treatment of health insurance!"

To be sure, there were some attempts by elected Republicans
to address health care, but those forays tended to involve aug-
menting the role of government. President Bush had a Repub-
lican-controlled Congress, and yet his major contribution in
the health care arena was to enact the Medicare prescription
drug program. Though the law contained some market-oriented features, it ultimately represented the largest expansion
of entitlements since the Great Society. At the state level,
Massachusetts Gov. Mitt Romney worked with the late liberal
icon Sen. Ted Kennedy in 2006 to pass a universal health care
program that would serve as the model for Obamacare. The
two laws even shared an architect – MIT economist Jonathan
Gruber – who has subsequently become infamous for videos
surfacing in which he admitted that Democrats obscured the
details of Obamacare in order to get it passed.[3]

Such attempts by Republicans to win on the left's playing field
reinforced the assumption on the right that any plan to address the issue of health care must necessarily entail expanding the role of government. In the long run, conservatives suf-
fered dearly for the inability of Republicans to advance free
market proposals when they had the power to do so.

---

3   See video: **https://www.youtube.com/watch?v=G790p0LcgbI**

During their time in the wilderness, smart liberals took lessons from their Clinton era defeat and refined their health care strategy in preparation for their next opening. By 2007, Democrats had retaken control of Congress and were widely expected to recapture the White House the following year. When the early campaigning started for the party's presidential nomination, liberal activists made it clear to the candidates that anybody who wanted to represent the party needed to have a universal health care proposal. Early on, the left even pilloried Obama for not articulating a sufficiently detailed vision.

Republicans didn't lose on health care when Obama won in 2008, or when he signed his bill into law in 2010, or even when the law survived a Supreme Court challenge and he was reelected in 2012. Republicans lost the health care debate when they failed to put in place a comprehensive free market plan when they were in charge.

But, contrary to what Obama likes to argue, the health care debate is not "over." It's here to stay. Within a decade, health care spending is expected to account for roughly one out of every five dollars of the U.S. economy[4] and the nation's major health programs are projected to cost the federal government nearly $13.8 trillion cumulatively over the coming 10-year

---

4   Klein, Philip. "Government actuaries see Obamacare driving up healthcare costs over the next decade." *Washington Examiner.* Sept. 3, 2014. http://www.washingtonexaminer.com/government-actuaries-see-obamacare-driving-up-healthcare-costs-over-next-decade/article/2552783

period.[5] Beyond the numbers, few issues are as deeply emotional to Americans as how they and their loved ones receive medical treatment. For these reasons and many others, health care is always going to have a starring role in the public policy debate.

Given that the health care debate will be a constant in American politics, the overarching question is: Will future Democratic administrations be able to build on Obamacare and increase the amount of centralized control of the health care system – or will future Republican administrations be able to change the current course and move the system in a free market direction? If conservatives want the latter scenario to pan out, they have to start coalescing around a plan of action.

The good news for opponents of President Obama's health care law is that a wide variety of alternative health care plans have emerged from lawmakers and thinkers on the right. The bad news is that there is currently no consensus on what would be the best way to tackle Obamacare, now that most of its major provisions have been implemented. "People are always saying, 'the Republicans have no replacement plans,'" remarked Sally Pipes, an influential health policy expert on the right. "Well, the problem is, they have too many plans."

Many of the differences among the competing proposals within the right-of-center health care policy community are

---

5 "An Update to the Budget and Economic Outlook: 2014 to 2024," Table 1-2. Congressional Budget Office. August 2014. http://www.cbo.gov/sites/default/files/45653-OutlookUpdate_2014_Aug.pdf

rooted in a principled disagreement over what the appropriate role is for government in the first place. Along this spectrum, some believe that there is a legitimate government role in making sure all Americans have access to some kind of affordable health coverage, while others argue that such a role is inappropriate and that policymakers should limit their focus to undoing distortionary government policies that drive up costs.

Regardless of what one believes philosophically, there is also a practical debate. Now that Obamacare has been implemented, whatever its problems, millions of Americans are receiving some kind of subsidized health coverage through the law. Given the historical durability of social welfare programs, this reality has triggered heated debates on the right about how much of the law is realistically in play and to what extent any alternative has to account for Obamacare's beneficiaries.

Though a number of proposals have grappled with these questions, the problem is that most Americans outside the narrow confines of the conservative health policy world don't have time to keep track of all the plans that have been churned out. But it's exactly those Americans who will be crucial to any effort to advance an alternative. This book, then, aims to distill the policy debate that has been playing out on the right into a concise and readable format.

In the chapters that follow, I will evaluate a range of ideas being offered on reforming the current health care system along free market lines, building on dozens of interviews with the politicians and thinkers at the center of the debate, and years of experience covering the issue. To be clear, this work isn't intended to be a detailed description of every aspect of every plan that's ever been offered by a conservative or libertarian health care expert. (If that were the case, I may as well direct readers to a stack of white papers and advertise the book as a natural cure for insomnia.) Instead, I will guide readers through the thinking that undergirds the various proposals, because ultimately, any technical policy decision is motivated by a broader guiding principle. Surveying the policy landscape on the right, I have grouped the various ideas being offered as alternatives to Obamacare into three basic approaches, or schools of thought.

The first approach comes from those who believe that fully repealing Obamacare is probably unrealistic, but who still see an opening to reform the overall health care system in a more market-oriented direction. I call this the Reform School.

The second approach comes from a crowd that believes full repeal is a necessity, but can only occur if opponents of the law create a market-friendly alternative with enough financial assistance to make health insurance widely available to those Americans who want to purchase it. I call this the Replace School.

And finally, there is a third approach, which advocates repealing the law, returning to pre-Obamacare levels of taxes and spending, and then using that clean slate as the basis to over-haul the system in a free market manner to bring down costs. I call this the Restart School.

"Not all Republicans agree on specifically how to replace Obamacare, but we do agree on many components of it," House Ways and Means Committee Chairman and 2012 vice presidential candidate Rep. Paul Ryan told me. "We all agree on a market-based, patient-centered system, but there are some design features that we have yet to get real consensus on… Over the next two years I believe we've got to show the country, 'Here's what an alternative to Obamacare looks like. Here's what repeal and replace looks like in 2017.'"[6]

Not every proposal explored in this book would require the full repeal of the law. But all of them, in some way, seek to reverse America's current trajectory toward a government takeover of health care and instead push the system in a more market-oriented direction.

Before getting into the plans themselves, it's important to ar-ticulate what I mean by a government takeover and a mar-ket-oriented health care system.

6   See video of the interview, which took place in Sept. 2014: http://www.wash-ingtonexaminer.com/article/2553760

Chapter 2
THE GOVERNMENT TAKEOVER

There are few things that will make liberals howl more than referring to President Obama's health care law as "a government takeover of health care." Given that I use the phrase in the title of this book, I thought it would be worth explaining more precisely what I mean.

The truth is that liberals have a point – but only up to a point. That is, Obamacare did not instantly transform the United States into Britain, where government offers health care to everybody, owns hospitals, employs doctors, and rations services. Nor was the system that existed in the U.S. prior to Obamacare anything close to a pure free market.

That having been said, Obamacare represents the largest expansion of the federal government's role in health care since the establishment of Medicare and Medicaid in 1965. And it represents a huge leap toward a single-payer style system in which government provides coverage to everybody and imposes system-wide cost controls.

It's no conspiracy to point out that Obama himself explicitly advocated a single-payer health care system. "I happen to be a proponent of a single-payer universal health care program," Obama said in a 2003 speech at a conference in Illinois sponsored by the AFL-CIO union. He went on to say,

"A single-payer health care plan, a universal health care plan. That's what I'd like to see. But as all of you know, we may not get there immediately. Because first we've got to take back the White House, we've got to take back the Senate, and we've got to take back the House."[7]

Although Obama, to use a presidential euphemism, "evolved" on the issue, he never philosophically abandoned the idea that single-payer was the ideal system. What differentiated him from the purists in his party was that he recognized that moving to a single-payer system overnight would have been too disruptive to the existing system and thus politically infeasible.

"If I were designing a system from scratch, then I'd probably set up a single-payer system," Obama said in response to an audience question during an August 2008 campaign event. "But the problem is we're not starting from scratch. We've got a system in which most people have become accustomed to getting their health insurance through their employer and for us to immediately transition from that and given that a lot of people work for insurance companies, a lot of people work for HMOs – you've got a whole system of institutions that have been set up. Making that transition in a rapid way I think would be very difficult."[8]

---

7   See video: https://www.youtube.com/watch?v=fpAyan1fXCE

8   See video: https://www.youtube.com/watch?v=l7wTDK-LwqE

Thus, what Obama and Congressional Democrats settled for when they gained power in Washington was moving the ball as far down field toward the ultimate single-payer goal as possible.

Initially, liberals pushed for a government-run plan to be offered on new insurance exchanges alongside privately administered plans. The theory was that a government-run plan would drive down costs because, compared to private insurers, it would have lower administrative costs and wouldn't need to make profits, and it could use its size to negotiate lower payment rates with medical providers. Liberals hoped – and conservatives feared – that this "public option" would be a way to migrate the system to single-payer over time.

During the fight to pass the law, Democrats were speaking to two audiences. They were trying to reassure moderates that the legislation was building on a market-based model, and thus attacked any suggestion by Republicans that what they were doing was anything akin to a government takeover of health care. But at the same time, they were trying to reassure liberals that the proposal made progress and therefore was worth supporting even though it maintained private insurance.

On Sept. 29, 2009, Sen. Max Baucus, D-Mont., who was one of the chief authors of Obamacare as chairman of the Finance Committee, explained his opposition to a public option.

Speaking as the committee voted on the provision,[9] Baucus explained that though he thought the idea had merits, his primary goal was to secure the 60 votes in the Senate needed to get the bill "across the finish line" and that this wouldn't be possible if a public option were included. But tellingly, he reassured liberals that the legislation shouldn't be seen as the end of the federal government's efforts to address health care.

"Rome wasn't built in a day," he said. "And only a few major pieces of legislation were totally complete when enacted." Baucus recalled that when President Roosevelt signed Social Security into law in 1935, he referred to the law as representing "'a cornerstone in a structure which is being built but is by no means complete.'"

Baucus continued, "That's what [Roosevelt] said. And we could also say that about this bill. We hope that it'll be the cornerstone of meaningful reform. I think it will be. But it is by no means a complete rewriting of the American health care system... The point is that today, this year, we need to start to lay that foundation."

In the end, liberals didn't get exactly what they wanted. The public option didn't survive the legislative process and the law enabled hundreds of billions of dollars of subsidies to flow through private insurance companies. But Democrats did end up laying that foundation.

---

9   "Senate Health Care Legislation Markup, Day 5, Part 3." C-Span archives. Sept. 29, 2009. http://www.c-span.org/video/?289202-2/ senate-health-care-legislation-markup-day-5-part-3

As passed, Obamacare added millions of Americans to the rolls of the government-run Medicaid and turned health insurance into a de facto public utility, capping the amount that insurers can earn in profits and spend on administrative costs relative to what they pay out in medical claims. The law compels individuals to purchase government-designed insurance policies under the threat of a penalty and subsidizes them to do so on government-run exchanges. It forces employers to purchase plans that meet requirements established by the federal government and imposes fines on businesses that do not comply.

As more time has elapsed since the bill's passage, liberals have been able to more openly acknowledge the fact that the law does represent a significant step toward a single-payer style system.

Consider this line: "The Affordable Care Act, aka Obamacare, is a policy Rube Goldberg device – instead of doing the simple, obvious thing, which would just be to insure everyone, it basically relies on a combination of regulations and subsidies to rope, coddle, and nudge us into a rough approximation of a single-payer system." Any conservative critic could have uttered most of that statement during the 2009-2010 health care debate. In reality, liberal New York Times columnist Paul Krugman wrote it in May 2013.[10]

---

10   Krugman, Paul. "Obamacare Will Be A Debacle – For Republicans." The New York Times. May 24, 2013. http://krugman.blogs.nytimes.com/2013/05/24/obamacare-will-be-a-debacle-for-republicans/

In a July 2014 blog post titled, "Stealth Single Payer," Krugman touted a study by the Kaiser Family Foundation showing that nearly three times as many Californians gaining coverage through Obamacare had done so through Medicaid as opposed to a privately administered exchange plan.[11]

"There have always been critics complaining that what we really should have is single-payer, and angry that subsidies were being funneled through the insurance companies," Krugman wrote. He reassured them: "it turns out that many of the newly insured are in fact being covered under a single-payer system – Medicaid."

He went on to note that Medicaid "is actually the piece of the US system that looks most like European health systems" and thus "liberals really should be celebrating" the program's expansion through Obamacare.

Sen. Harry Reid, D-Nev., who helped muscle Obamacare through the Senate when he was majority leader, admitted quite openly that it was his view that the U.S. would eventually do away with private insurance altogether.

Asked by Steve Sebelius of the *Las Vegas Review-Journal* in August 2013 why Democrats didn't push a single-payer plan, Reid said, "Don't think that we didn't have a tremendous number of people who wanted a single-payer system," but, he

11   Krugman, Paul. "Stealth Single Payer." *The New York Times.* July 30, 2014. http://krugman.blogs.nytimes.com/2014/07/30/stealth-single-payer/

explained, there weren't enough votes for a single-payer system or a public option.[12]

Referring to the current insurance-based model in the U.S. which Obamacare left intact, Reid said, "I think we have to work our way past that." After recounting the history and development of the system, Reid said, "What we've done here with Obamacare is a step in the right direction, but we're far from having something that's going to work forever."

When Sebelius followed up to clarify that Reid envisioned an eventual end to the U.S. insurance model, he responded, "Yes. Absolutely, yes."

It's easy to see how Reid could be so optimistic. With Medicaid expanding, Medicare growing rapidly as Baby Boomers retire, and millions of Americans gaining subsidized insurance through the Obamacare exchanges, government-sponsored health coverage will be responsible for nearly half of the nation's $5.3 trillion[13] in health care spending by 2023,

---

12   Demirjian, Karoun. "Reid says Obamacare just a step toward eventual single-payer system." *Las Vegas Sun.* Aug. 10, 2013. http://www.lasvegassun.com/ news/2013/aug/10/reid-says-obamacare-just-step-toward-eventual-sing/

See also video: https://www.youtube.com/watch?v=SXgSKwYMnWo

13   Sisko, Andrea, et al. "National Health Expenditure Projections, 2013-23: Faster Growth Expected With Expanded Coverage And Improving Economy." *Health Affairs* online edition. September 2014. http://content.healthaffairs.org/ content/33/10/1841

according to actuaries from the Centers for Medicare and Medicaid Services.[14]

The undeniable reality is that, unless there is a serious policy response from the right, America will continue to morph into a single-payer health care system, with future Democratic administrations adding to the "cornerstone" erected by Obamacare.

---

14 But these numbers actually understate the government's role. The CMS numbers categorize as "private" taxes and premiums paid toward Medicare as well as individual contributions toward premiums for insurance purchased through one of Obamacare's exchanges. Beyond that, the numbers themselves don't account for the qualitative role now played by the federal government, such as dictating to individuals and businesses the type of coverage they must purchase.

Chapter 3
HAVING HEALTH CARE YOUR WAY

I'll never forget the time that a Londoner told me she enjoyed McDonald's but found it annoying that they put pickles on their burgers. I responded with what was evidently a radical solution: "Why not just not order yours without pickles?" Looking at me as if I had just floated in the air on a hover board, she replied, "You can do that?"

Admittedly, bringing up fast food in the context of a discussion about free market health solutions may seem strange. But if you'll humor me for a minute, the main point that struck me about that exchange was how it was second nature to me that people should order fast food just as they wanted it while it didn't even occur to my British counterpart.

My expectation that it was practically a God-given right to control what goes on my burger is not an accident. In 1974, Burger King, seeking to gain market share on its much larger rival, launched its "Have it your way" advertising campaign, exploiting the streamlined process of McDonald's to offer its customers more control over their burgers.[15] In a 60-second commercial, a family walks into a Burger King and the dad asks if it's okay to order a Whopper without pickles or lettuce, and the cashier sings, in a classic advertising jingle: "Hold the

---

15   North, Deb. "Mass Customization." *QSR* magazine. **http://www2.qsrmagazine.com/articles/features/104/customization-1.phtml**

pickle, hold the lettuce/Special orders don't upset us/All that we ask is that you let us/Serve it your way."[16] The challenge posed by Burger King, in turn, eventually prompted McDonald's to become more accommodating.

This one skirmish in the long-running fast food burger wars is part of a much larger tradition in America. Throughout U.S. economic history, Americans have demanded that businesses cater to their individual needs. In response, businesses have competed aggressively with one another for customers, and in the process of doing so, have driven down costs and expanded choice – often improving quality as well.

In 1946, the Radio Corporation of America unveiled a new 10-inch black and white television at a time when only a few channels were regularly broadcasting.[17] The price was $350, or $4,272, adjusted for inflation.[18]

Today, for around the same inflation-adjusted cost, an American consumer could visit the Best Buy website and purchase nine 50-inch Sharp high-definition color flat screens, which could be used to access hundreds of channels, stream movies, or play video games.

Examples of technological advancements lowering costs while improving quality extend well beyond televisions – to

---

16   See video: https://www.youtube.com/watch?v=KJXzkUH72cY

17   http://www.earlytelevision.org/pdf/rca-630ts-rider-tv1.pdf

18   This estimate was derived from the Bureau of Labor Statistics CPI Inflation Calculator tool: http://www.bls.gov/data/inflation_calculator.htm

computing, transportation, communication and a litany of other areas.

Even in an area like fast food, which isn't exactly known for ushering in a new era of culinary quality, major chains have introduced healthier options as awareness builds about the detrimental health impacts of processed foods. We've seen the rise of smaller burger chains that use fresh – rather than frozen – ingredients, to offer more choice to individuals who want to avoid the processed quality of major fast food chains.

But there's one prominent area in which the U.S. does not have anything approaching a functioning consumer market, and where instead, the consumer is completely left in the dark, given few choices, elbowed out of the decision-making process by large bureaucracies, and given very little incentive to seek out the best deal. Unfortunately, this area accounts for $2.9 trillion in spending, representing more than one-sixth of the U.S. economy.[19] I am, of course, referring to health care.

Government has long been creating barriers to the formation of a free market for health care in America. Obamacare built many more of them.

In the U.S. health care system, those over 65 are eligible for a fiscally unsustainable, government-run, one size fits all,

---

19   Hartman, Micah, et al. "National Health Spending In 2013: Growth Slows, Remains In Step With the Overall Economy." *Health Affairs* online edition. December 2014. http://content.healthaffairs.org/content/early/2014/11/25/hlthaff.2014.1107

Medicare program. Those who have low enough incomes can obtain health coverage through Medicaid.

In fiscal year 2013, states and the federal government spent nearly $460 billion on Medicaid, and yet, an extensive study done in Oregon and published in the *New England Journal of Medicine* in 2013 found that gaining coverage through the program wasn't associated with a significant measured improvement in physical health outcomes.[20] Due to the fact that Medicaid pays doctors so little, it offers limited access to care. An investigation conducted by the Inspector General for the Department of Health and Human Services revealed that "slightly more than half of providers could not offer appointments to enrollees" – and that was among doctors who were listed as participating in Medicaid. The investigation was conducted in 2013, before Obamacare added millions of Americans to the broken program.[21]

In addition, Obamacare set up a vehicle, known as exchanges, through which lower-income individuals can purchase insurance using government subsidies. But the insurance plans offered on the exchanges are more costly than they need to be and don't offer a genuine choice to consumers, because every plan has to meet specifications of the federal government.

20   Baicker, Katherine, et al. "The Oregon Experiment – Effects of Medicaid on Clinical Outcomes." *The New England Journal of Medicine.* May 2, 2013. **http:// www.nejm.org/doi/full/10.1056/NEJMsa1212321**

21   "Access to Care: Provider Availability in Medicaid Managed Care." Department of Health and Human Services. December 2014. **http://oig.hhs.gov/oei/ reports/oei-02-13-00670.pdf**

Most Americans who don't qualify for public assistance obtain insurance through their employers. To provide a bit of history, the explosion of employer-based insurance started during World War II, when the government imposed wage controls. To attract talent, businesses responded by offering benefits instead, which were excluded from those compensation limits.[22] The IRS subsequently ruled that health insurance premiums could be paid by employers on a tax-exempt basis. Meaning, any insurance purchased through one's employer could be paid for with pre-tax money.

People are so accustomed to the employer-based system by now that they rarely think of its downsides. But there are many. To start, if employers weren't providing insurance, they'd be able to pay workers higher salaries. Some workers might just prefer to have the extra cold hard cash over whatever health insurance policy their employer decides to pick for them. Which brings up another downside of the employer-based system.

Individuals who receive their insurance through their employers are typically limited to choosing among – at most – a few plans. Those workers might prefer to purchase cheaper plans and have more money left over for other expenses, or they might be willing to pay more for plans that offer a wider range of doctors. But, in the system as it exists today, they have to settle for the plan their employers have chosen. Fur-

---

22 "Employer-Sponsored Health Insurance and Health Reform." National Bureau of Economic Research. http://www.nber.org/bah/2009no2/w14839.html

thermore, those individuals who are satisfied with their employer plans have to face the prospect of changing their coverage if they switch jobs, which is quite common in today's work force.

When you add up Medicare, Medicaid, Obamacare, and employment-based insurance, roughly 95 percent of those insured in the U.S. are covered either through the government or their employers, and thus have little control over their health insurance options.[23]

But it isn't as if individuals outside of this system have genuine choices, either. To start, they don't get the same tax benefit as those obtaining insurance through their employers. So instead of buying insurance out of their gross earnings, they have to pay all their taxes, and purchase insurance out of the smaller amount of money that's left over. Because the tax code has discriminated against individuals purchasing insurance on their own for decades, the individual market was always relatively small and volatile as people moved in and out of it as they lost or gained employment or government benefits. As a result, there was never an opportunity for the development of a strong and stable market for individuals to purchase health insurance.

In addition, even before Obamacare, there were still over 2,000 health coverage mandates being imposed at the state level, according to the Council for Affordable Health Insur-

---

23   "Health Insurance Coverage of the Total Population." 2013. Kaiser Family Foundation. **http://kff.org/other/state-indicator/total-population/**

ance, which estimated the mandates helped drive up the cost of basic insurance by as high as 50 percent in some states.[24] These coverage mandates included requirements that all insurance policies cover treatments ranging from prostate cancer screening and mammography to morbid obesity treatment, or breast reduction surgery (required in Maine). On the surface, it might be seen as a good thing that many states wanted to make sure that insurance coverage was comprehensive. But the flip side of dictating the type of insurance individuals must purchase is that the government is denying individuals the ability to purchase insurance that meets their particular needs.

This doesn't have to be the case. Most forms of insurance are used to protect individuals against major losses. Homeowners' insurance, for example, will cover the cost of a tree damaging the roof in the event of a major storm, but it does not cover visits by the plumber. Car insurance will cover damages from accidents, but not oil changes or gas fill ups. Yet with health insurance, there's been an expectation created by government policy that it should cover the costs of routine expenses, which necessarily makes premiums higher than they otherwise could be.

A young and healthy individual might prefer to purchase a less comprehensive plan with lower monthly premiums as

---

24   Craig Bunce, Victoria and Wieske, J.P. "Health Insurance Mandates in the States 2009." Council for Affordable Health Insurance. http://www.cbia.com/ ieb/ag/CostOfCare/RisingCosts/CAHI_HealthInsuranceMandates2009.pdf

long as it offered financial coverage if something catastrophic happened. Or a 60-year old woman might not want to pay for an insurance policy that includes infertility treatment. What the government is doing by imposing mandates is the equivalent of saying that those who want to purchase a car have to buy a Porsche or no car at all.

To demonstrate how much regulations can drive up costs, in 2012, the average annual premium of an individual health insurance plan in New York was $4,260 per year, according to eHealth, which sells insurance online. That same year, the cost of an average policy in the neighboring (but less regulated) state of Pennsylvania was $2,088, or less than half that amount.[25] This is why many Republican proposals before Obamacare called for allowing the interstate purchase of insurance, thus giving individuals in highly regulated states access to more affordable options being offered elsewhere. Obamacare made that impossible.

The one redeeming factor of the individual market before Obamacare was that regulations were being passed at the state level, so people in some states still had affordable coverage if they wanted it, even if that option wasn't available in heavily regulated states. But Obamacare imposed onerous regulations at the federal level, driving up costs and limiting choices everywhere.

25   "Cost and Benefits of Individual and Family Health Insurance." eHealth. December 2013. http://news.ehealthinsurance.com/_ir/68/201311/eHealth%20 2013%20Cost%20and%20Benefits%20Report.pdf

As an example, in Arizona in 2013 (the year before Obamacare's major provisions kicked in) a 30-year old single male non-smoker could purchase insurance for as cheaply as $456 over the course of the year, according to a study by the Government Accountability Office.[26] But in 2015, the cheapest plan available on the Obamacare Healthcare.gov exchange for a 30 year-old non-smoker in Arizona (after a search of multiple zip codes) was $1,620 annually.

Even this staggering difference understates the burden of Obamacare. In the pre-Obamacare world, individuals who didn't want to purchase insurance could simply choose to go without it. But Obamacare forces individuals to purchase insurance or pay a financial penalty. By 2016, the penalty for going uninsured will be $695, or 2.5 percent of taxable income, whichever is greater.[27]

Supporters of the law would passionately respond by noting that the law also offers generous subsidies so low-income individuals won't have to pay anywhere near the full sticker price of insurance. The problem is, relying on taxpayers to pick up the tab for inflated insurance significantly drives up spending. The law spends over $1 trillion of taxpayer money

---

26   Letter to Sen. Orrin Hatch. "Private Health Insurance: The Range of Base Premiums in the Individual Market by State in January 2013." GAO. http://www.gao.gov/assets/660/656121.pdf

27   "Individual Mandate Q&A." Aetna. https://www.aetna.com/health-reform-connection/questions-answers/individual-mandate.html

subsidizing individuals to purchase insurance, and another $800 billion on expanding Medicaid.[28]

It's also worth noting that insurance premiums would have risen even further under Obamacare, but one way that insurers responded to the new regulatory environment was to contain costs by dropping doctors and hospitals out of their coverage networks, meaning fewer choices for consumers. The problem has been so bad in California that it has already provoked a spate of lawsuits.[29]

In addition to these problems being exacerbated by Obamacare, the American health care system suffers from inflated prices, because individuals have no way of knowing how much services cost and usually little reason to care. Individuals go to their doctors' offices or hospitals, throw down their private or government insurance cards, and either most of the bills get paid leaving them with small fees, or, maybe they get outrageous bills that they can't quite comprehend. This is the opposite of how a true market system should work.

There are two key components of a functioning consumer market – that individuals have control over their own money and that there is a way to compare value. Give consumers

---

28   "Updated Estimates of the Effects of the Insurance Coverage Provisions of the Affordable Care Act." Congressional Budget Office. April 2014. https://www.cbo.gov/publication/45231

29   Terhune, Chad et al. "Obamacare doctor networks to stay limited in 2015." *Los Angeles Times.* Sept. 28, 2014. http://www.latimes.com/business/la-fi-0928-obamacare-doctors-20140928-story.html#page=1

the motivation they need to save money and the information they need to do so, and suppliers of goods and services will respond by providing better value. For the most part, neither feature exists in the American health care system.

When consumers know that their government or employer health policy will cover a medical service, they have little reason to seek a better deal or consider whether a given service is really necessary.

Even for those who want to shop around, there is a staggering lack of transparency. A person could land in any city in America and quickly research the best restaurants in her price range by consulting an effectively limitless number of resources. The same is true for purchasing a new smart phone, or oven, or lawnmower, or any of a number of consumer items. But it's about as easy to find a three-legged ballerina[30] as to get comparable information about price and outcomes from local doctors and hospitals. Is it any wonder why the U.S. medical system is so expensive?

The goal of most free market plans for overhauling the health care system involve thinking of reforms to the patchwork of existing government policies to transform the Frankenstein monster of American health care into a system that fosters a consumer market. The thinking is that by unleashing discriminating American consumers on the medical system and giving them more control and choices, the resulting compe-

---

30   See John Candy joke in *Planes, Trains, and Automobiles,* directed by John Hughes (1987, Paramount Pictures).

tition would improve quality and lower prices just as in other aspects of the economy.

For instance, imagine a system in which individuals wouldn't have to accept whatever insurance their employers offered, because they'd enjoy the same tax status if they decided to buy plans of their own. Individually purchased insurance would be attached to them rather than any given employer, so they wouldn't have to fret about losing their insurance if they lost or changed jobs.

The portability would also motivate insurers to provide incentives for healthier behavior. In the current system in which many Americans change jobs (and thus insurance) every few years, insurers have no reason to care if a beneficiary smokes, eats unhealthily, or doesn't exercise. But if insurers know that people who sign up for insurance at 25 could conceivably be their customers for the next 40 years, they have a much greater reason to take an interest in people's long-term health and develop financial rewards for healthy behaviors (much like car insurers will, say, offer discounts after a certain period of safe driving).

Wipe away the mountain of mandates placed on health insurance, and individuals in this system would have a wider range of choices of health plans available to them at a lower cost. And because individuals would have more control over their health care dollars, they'd be more motivated to seek out better and cheaper care.

Critics of this approach often argue that it's unrealistic to expect that Americans – who spend countless hours researching new car purchases – would actually want to behave like consumers when it comes to health care. After all, a person in an ambulance with a heart attack isn't going to start researching the best and cheapest care available. But this is mostly a red herring – in 2012, emergency room services accounted for just 2 percent of U.S. health care spending.[31]

In more typical cases, evidence has shown that Americans will shop for a better deal on health care if given an incentive and the tools to do so. For instance, a study published by the *Journal of the American Medical Association* in October 2014 looked at more than 500,000 individuals who were covered by 18 large employers and were granted access to a platform, Castlight Health, that allowed them to compare prices among medical providers either by phone or online.[32]

31 Medical Expenditure Panel Survey. "Table 6: Emergency Room Services-Median and Mean Expenses per Person With Expense and Distribution of Expenses by Source of Payment: United States, 2012 Facility And SBD Expenses" Agency for Healthcare Research and Quality, U.S. Department of Health and Human Services.

http://meps.ahrq.gov/mepsweb/data_stats/tables_compendia_hh_interactive.jsp?_SERVICE=MEPSSocket0&_PROGRAM=MEPSPGM. TC.SAS&File=HCFY2012&Table=HCFY2012_PLEXP_E&VAR1=AGE&-VAR2=SEX&VAR3=RACETH5C&VAR4=INSURCOV&VAR5=POV-CAT12&VAR6=MSA&VAR7=REGION&VAR8=HEALTH&-VARO1=4+17+44+64&VARO2=1&VARO3=1&VARO4=1&VARO5=1&-VARO6=1&VARO7=1&VARO8=1&_Debug=

32 Whaley, Christopher, et al. "Association Between Availability of Health Service Prices and Payments for These Services." *The Journal of the American*

Researchers found that individuals who used the platform had claims payments that were 14 percent lower for lab tests, 13 percent lower for more advanced imaging such as MRIs or CT scans, and a more modest 1 percent lower for doctors' visits. The savings on advanced imaging translated into a dollar value of $125 per service.

There are, no doubt, limitations to the study. For one thing, not all medical services an individual may receive lend themselves to clear price information. But the research does present compelling evidence of the potential for the health care system to function as a market if consumers are given the proper incentives and sufficient information. Even savings that seem modest, applied for many services across the medical system, could make a big difference.

Another pocket of the health care system where the possibilities of consumer-directed health care have shown promise is with high-deductible health plans. High-deductible health plans carry lower premiums and are often combined with health savings accounts, which allow individuals to pay for routine medical expenses with pre-tax dollars, giving them more control over their money and greater flexibility in choosing which doctors they see.

Between 2005 and 2013, the number of Americans with HSA connected high-deductible health plans rose from 1 million

---

Medical Association. Oct. 22-29, 2014. http://jama.jamanetwork.com/article.aspx?articleid=1917438

to 15.5 million.[33] Actuaries at the Center for Medicare and Medicaid Services said that the increased use of such plans was one factor in slowing the growth of private health insurance spending.[34] Not only are the premiums cheaper, but because consumers have to spend more on health care before their insurance company starts pitching in (i.e., before they hit their deductible), they have a greater incentive to avoid seeking unnecessary care. That's a much more sustainable way to contain spending over time than top down cost controls common in government dominated plans.

A health care market in which consumers have the ability to shop around would also pressure providers to improve their customer service – a welcome change from a system in which individuals often feel like they are herded around like sheep.

Finally, a more dynamic and innovative system would be a better fit with the historical American character. Citizens of other countries with more collectivist traditions may find socialized systems acceptable, but a system worthy of American culture would be one in which the consumer is king.

---

33   America's Health Insurance Plans. "January 2013 Census Shows 15.5 Million People Covered by Health Savings Account/High-Deductible Health Plans (HAS/HDHPs)." June 2013. http://www.ahip.org/HSA2013/

34   Klein, Philip. "Consumer-driven healthcare a more sustainable way to contain spending." *Washington Examiner.* Dec. 5, 2014. http://www.washingtonexaminer.com/consumer-driven-healthcare-a-more-sustainable-way-to-contain-spending/article/2557006

The question that all of the plans in this book attempt to confront is: How do we get as close as possible to this free market vision in a post-Obamacare world?

Chapter 4
THE REFORM SCHOOL

In the summer and fall of 2013, when Sen. Ted Cruz, R-Tex, led the ultimately failed effort to defund Obamacare, one of his central arguments was that if Republicans didn't seize the moment to block the law, they would never again be able to get rid of it. His rationale was that once Americans started receiving subsidies through the law on Jan. 1, 2014, the program would quickly become entrenched, just like other major federal entitlements.

"[I]n modern times, no major entitlement has ever been implemented and then unwound," Cruz told the *Daily Caller* in Aug. 2013.[35]

Cruz said at a Tea Party gathering that same month, "[Obama's] strategy is to get as many Americans as possible hooked on the subsidies, addicted to the sugar. If we get to Jan. 1, this thing is here forever."[36]

---

35   Pappas, Alex. "4 Questions with Ted Cruz on defunding Obamacare." *The Daily Caller.* Aug. 15, 2013. http://dailycaller.com/2013/08/15/4-questions-with-ted-cruz-on-defunding-obamacare/

36   Root, Jay. "Cruz: Americans Could Get 'Addicted' to Obamacare." *The Texas Tribune.* Aug. 19, 2013. http://www.texastribune.org/2013/08/19/cruz-warns-americans-could-get-addicted-obamacare/

On another occasion, he told Laura Ingraham that, "If this goes into effect on Jan. 1, we will never, ever, ever get rid of it."[37]

Though the exact number of Americans receiving benefits through Obamacare is the subject of some debate, it can now be said that millions of Americans are obtaining health coverage through the law, either as a result of its Medicaid expansion or through its subsidized exchanges. And the number is only expected to grow by 2017, the earliest Republicans would realistically be in a position to fully repeal the law were the party to take over the White House.

As a whole, Obamacare remains undeniably unpopular, but that doesn't necessarily mean that the public is eager for it to be entirely scrapped, either. This was something that could be seen even during the disastrous rollout of the program's Healthcare.gov insurance website. In early Dec. 2013, in the midst of the bungled launch, a Gallup poll found that just 17 percent of respondents wanted to keep the law "as is." But at the same time, only 32 percent supported repealing the law entirely.[38]

So, if the arguments Cruz was making in the fall of 2013 are correct and the polling numbers suggesting public trepida-

---

37   McCormack, John. "Never Surrender." *The Weekly Standard*. Sept. 30, 2013. http://www.weeklystandard.com/articles/never-surrender_756465.html

38   Swift, Art. "Majority of Americans Want Major Changes to Health Law." Dec. 6, 2013. http://www.gallup.com/poll/166145/majority-americans-major-changes-health-law.aspx

tion about full repeal are accurate, what are opponents of Obamacare to do?

One approach is to propose reforms that move Obamacare in a more market-oriented direction without necessarily repealing the entire law. This is the thinking of the Reform School.

Such an approach could be pursued through a large overhaul bill, or in a series of smaller pieces. In lieu of full repeal, in other words, Republicans could pass more targeted legislation that eliminates parts of the law.

For instance, Republicans could get rid of the unpopular mandates forcing individuals and employers to purchase government-approved insurance coverage. Scrapping the individual mandate would expand liberty and eliminate an expensive burden for Americans. Getting rid of the employer mandate would remove the incentive for businesses to curtail hiring or cut back workers' hours to avoid costly penalties for failing to provide coverage the government deems acceptable.

Additionally, Republicans could pass legislation eliminating a litany of taxes imposed by Obamacare that come to roughly $1 trillion[39] over a decade – such as taxes on medical devices, health insurance premiums, pharmaceuticals, and investment income.

---

39   "Letter to the Honorable John Boehner providing an estimate for H.R. 6079, the Repeal of Obamacare Act." The Congressional Budget Office. July 24, 2012. https://www.cbo.gov/publication/43471

They could also unravel a web of regulations that have worked to drive up the cost of insurance by forcing younger and healthier individuals to pay for more expensive insurance policies to help subsidize coverage for older and sicker beneficiaries. The law's exchanges could be deregulated, so that there are fewer restrictions on what types of insurance can be offered, to provide for more choices to consumers. Other reforms could turn over more power to the states to implement the health care law in a way that makes sense for their populations.

Grace-Marie Turner, who founded the Galen Institute in 1995 to promote free market health care policies and has regularly consulted with Republicans on Capitol Hill, said she favored a step-by-step approach to undoing Obamacare, which she argued was already showing some signs of success.

She noted that since Republicans assumed control of the House of Representatives in 2011, Speaker John Boehner, R-Ohio, has been able to pick off elements of Obamacare. For instance, Republicans were able to repeal a burdensome provision that required businesses to report transactions of at least $600 to the IRS. Republicans were also able to secure a repeal of another entitlement within Obamacare known as the CLASS Act. In theory, the CLASS Act was supposed to be able to provide long-term care benefits to those who paid premiums, but when the Department of Health and Human Services started trying to implement the program, they found it wasn't viable. An HHS analysis determined that there was no way that the program would generate enough premium income to finance the generous benefits. Though HHS suspended the CLASS Act, the program was still technically on the books, so by negotiating a deal to repeal it, Republicans ensured that it couldn't be resurrected.[40]

"You aren't going to see a big plan," said Turner. "Because [Republicans] know that's not the way you go about it. You go about dealing with a step-by-step approach so you can set the stage for the kinds of reforms that you would do if a Republican were in the White House."

Even if a Republican is elected in 2016, however, she said she doesn't think full repeal is in the cards.

"I think there is a growing realization that you are not going to repeal the whole thing until, at the earliest 2017, at which time the industry will have been organizing itself around this law, because they had no other choice for seven years," she said. "And so, there will have been structural changes in our health sector that cannot be undone, that require a more strategic and I think more surgical approach."

She added, "There's a reality that seven years into this, it makes it very hard to repeal a law that has so many tentacles and deep roots."

As Republicans scrapped elements of the law, she said, they could work toward injecting more free market features into

40   Spoerry, Scott. "Obama drops long-term care program." CNN. Oct. 17, 2011. http://www.cnn.com/2011/10/14/politics/health-care-program/

the system. She described it as, "much more of an evolutionary kind of approach than an unplug-and-replace kind of approach." Another benefit she sees of this line of attack is that Republicans can use each bill targeting a portion of Obamacare as an opportunity to further educate Americans about detrimental aspects of the law of which they may not have been aware.

Pursuing such a piecemeal approach would raise a number of issues, however. Obamacare is a complex law with many interlocking parts. Removing one part without attacking it in a more comprehensive way would risk having ripple effects. Getting rid of the individual mandate without making other changes, for instance, could destabilize the insurance market and drive up premiums as younger and healthier individuals would be less motivated to purchase coverage. That could leave insurers with disproportionately older and sicker enrollees, because, barring broader changes to Obamacare, insurers would still be legally required to cover individuals with pre-existing conditions.

Jettisoning the employer mandate while preserving generous subsidies for individuals to purchase insurance could discourage businesses from offering coverage. If businesses were to dump their workers on government-run exchanges instead, it would impose additional health care costs on taxpayers.

In addition, repealing the taxes in Obamacare without eliminating the spending they were intended to finance would mean that the program would add to deficits.

Even putting such considerations aside, a number of conservatives have also feared that an incremental approach would represent bad strategy by weakening the political constituency for making broader changes to the law. Given that the coalition opposing Obamacare is comprised of a number of groups with objections to certain elements of the law, chipping away at the program to remove some of these objectionable pieces could erode opposition. For instance, get rid of the employer mandate, and businesses who are currently fighting the requirement may find it easier to make peace with the law.

But Turner dismissed such concerns as outdated. At this point, she said, "There's no choice but to do an incremental approach." She said Americans, "don't want a big gigantic replacement plan. That scares them."

Like Turner, Manhattan Institute health policy scholar Avik Roy, who also worked as an adviser on Mitt Romney's 2012 presidential campaign, is skeptical that Obamacare can be fully repealed and believes that market-oriented reformers must recognize this reality. But counter to Turner's warnings about introducing giant proposals, in August 2014, Roy released a sweeping plan to overhaul the health care system.[41]

---

41   Roy, Avik. "Transcending Obamacare: A Patient-Centered Plan for Near-Universal Coverage and Permanent Fiscal Solvency." Manhattan Institute. August 2014. http://www.manhattan-institute.org/html/mpr_17.htm#.VIOLV1fF_48

"While I want it to achieve conservative goals, my most important goal being solving the fiscal problems we have, I also want to make sure that it can actually pass the Senate," Roy said. "If you want to give it a fighting chance, unless Republicans are going to get 60 Senators anytime soon, you gotta be able to throw a bone to these centrist Democrats." Roy was referring to the 60 votes required to overcome any attempt by the minority party to block legislation through a filibuster.

Roy's philosophical starting point on the health care issue differs from that of many conservatives in that he has argued in favor of universal coverage, calling it "a morally worthy goal."[42] His plan is also based on the assumption that repeal is unlikely.

His overarching idea is for Republicans to perform what he's referred to as a "jiu-jitsu" maneuver. In short, he has proposed that Republicans reform Obamacare to make it more market friendly and then use that modified structure to achieve broader reforms to the nation's older health care entitlements.

Health care spending remains the biggest driver of the nation's long-term debt problem and "substantial changes" are required to government health programs to put the nation on a sustainable financial footing, according to the Congressio-

---

42   Roy, Avik. "A Conservative Case for Universal Coverage." *Washington Examiner.* Jan. 17, 2014. http://www.washingtonexaminer.com/a-conservative-case-for-universal-coverage/article/2542091

nal Budget Office.[43] By 2024, one out of three dollars collected in federal tax revenue will be consumed by Medicare and Medicaid alone.[44] This statistic doesn't even count the additional money that is spent by state governments on Medicaid (the program is actually the biggest component of state budgets, according to the National Association of State Budget Officers).[45]

Reforming Medicare and Medicaid has been a goal of conservatives for decades, and changes to the programs were the centerpiece of all of the budgets that Republicans have passed since taking over the House of Representatives in 2011. Rep. Paul Ryan, R-Wis., during his time as chairman of the House Budget Committee between 2011 and 2014, sought to put the nation on a sustainable fiscal trajectory by transitioning Medicare into a system in which seniors could choose from a number of competing health insurance plans on a government exchange. His plan also gave states more flexibility over how to implement Medicaid for low-income Americans.

---

43 "The 2014 Long-Term Budget Outlook." Congressional Budget Office. July 14, 2014. https://www.cbo.gov/publication/45471

44 "An Update to the Budget and Economic Outlook: 2014 to 2024." Table 1-2. Congressional Budget Office. August 2014. http://www.cbo.gov/sites/default/files/45653-OutlookUpdate_2014_Aug.pdf

45 "State Expenditure Report: Examining Fiscal 2012-2014 State Spending." National Association of State Budget Officers. http://www.nasbo.org/sites/default/files/State%20Expenditure%20Report%20%28Fiscal%202012-2014%29S.pdf

Some people have charged that it's contradictory for Republicans to, on one hand, attack Obamacare's insurance exchanges, and on the other hand, support moving Medicare recipients into another kind of exchange. But it's a matter of perspective. Relative to a freer market, having the government set up an exchange through which it subsidizes individuals to purchase coverage is a step toward bigger government. But Medicare is already a government-run, single-payer style health care program. So, comparatively speaking, creating an exchange that gives seniors at least some modicum of choice and control over their own money would at least inject some market principles into it.

Given this reality, Roy's approach aims to kill two birds with one stone – to reform Obamacare's exchanges and then use them as a way to implement long-sought structural reforms to Medicare and Medicaid. "The goal should be to solve the long-term problem with minimal disruption to people's current health care arrangements," he said.

Roy doesn't think any alternative to Obamacare stands a chance politically if it doesn't aim to preserve at least similar coverage levels, because otherwise there would be a huge backlash, with the news dominated by stories of low-income Americans or individuals with pre-existing conditions losing their insurance.

Roy would make a number of changes to Obamacare's exchanges intended to increase choice and lower premiums. His plan would allow insurers to charge older Americans more for insurance – meaning a lighter burden would be placed on younger Americans.

In addition, he would scrap many of the law's taxes, subsidize health savings accounts, and encourage higher-deductible plans. These moves are all intended to give Americans more control over how their health care dollars are spent, motivating them to seek out more cost effective care. He would offer insurance subsidies to individuals earning up to roughly $37,000 in 2014 dollars (Obamacare offers subsidies to those earning up to about $47,000).[46]

His plan, like Obamacare, would force insurers to cover those with pre-existing conditions and prevent them from charging different rates based on enrollees' health statuses. But at the same time, he would scrap the mandate requiring that individuals purchase coverage or pay a penalty, which is the central way that the law aims to prod younger and healthier Americans into purchasing insurance. Attracting younger and healthier individuals with low medical costs into the insurance market is necessary to offset the costs to insurers of covering older and sicker patients. To make sure insurers

---

46 Roy's plan offers subsidies to those earning 317 percent of the federal poverty level. Obamacare's subsidies go up to 400 percent of the federal poverty level. The federal poverty level is a measure updated by the Department of Health and Human Services each year that sets the guidelines for who is considered to be living in poverty for the purposes of federal benefit programs. In 2014, the federal poverty level for a single individual was $11,670. See here for more information: **http:// aspe.hhs.gov/poverty/14poverty.cfm**

have the right batch of enrollees without a mandate, Roy suggests a two-pronged approach.

First, Roy's research found that age was the biggest driver of variations in health costs among the population. That is, even though there are old and healthy individuals and young and sick individuals, those cases aren't numerous enough compared to the population as a whole to substantially affect insurers' calculations.

Given this, Roy determined that by allowing insurers to charge older Americans six times as much for health insurance as younger Americans (as opposed to Obamacare's three-to-one limit), insurers would generate enough premium revenue to maintain a stable market without a mandate – even if they were still required to offer coverage to people with pre-existing conditions.

Under Obamacare's three-to-one ratio, premiums have soared for younger Americans. Average premiums for 23 year-old men were up 78.2 percent in 2014, the first year of Obamacare's implementation, when compared to 2013, according to a study from HealthPocket.com.[47] The increase was lower for women of the same age, but still a steep 44.9 percent.

---

47   Klein, Philip. "All ages see higher premiums under Obamacare." *Washington Examiner.* Nov. 3, 2014. http://www.washingtonexaminer.com/all-ages-see-higher-premiums-under-obamacare/article/2555546

Allowing for the six-to-one variation would significantly reduce premiums relative to Obamacare for younger Americans, giving them more incentive to purchase insurance, which would also help insurers maintain a functional market.

"There are typically younger people who are uninsured, because insurance is too expensive relative to their actual health risks," Roy said. "If you really want to make a dent in the uninsured population, the goal shouldn't be to make insurance more expensive for young people. It should be to make insurance less expensive for young people."

In addition, Roy's plan would replace the current annual open enrollment period with a limited six-week period every two years. In other words, those who choose to forgo insurance coverage would have to wait up to two years for their next opportunity to obtain insurance coverage if they incur unexpected medical expenses, giving them a strong incentive to sign up for coverage.

Roy's proposal would get rid of some, but not all, of Obamacare's taxes. Taxes on drug makers, medical device manufacturers, and a broader tax on the insurance industry would be scrapped. He would also repeal the employer mandate. But he would maintain Obamacare's "Cadillac Tax" on benefit-heavy employer health plans and even move up its effective date by a year, to 2017. This is one move intended to discourage the prevalence of generous health plans that insulate individuals from having any notion of the true cost of their care and encourage overspending.

As far as broader entitlement reform, Roy's proposal would gradually move Medicare beneficiaries over to the reformed Obamacare exchanges. He would achieve this by increasing the retirement age from its current 65 by four months every year. So, while the reform wouldn't affect existing retirees, each year, a new cohort of seniors would be getting their insurance through the exchanges as opposed to traditional Medicare. To demonstrate: after 9 years, the retirement age would go up to 68; after 30 years, individuals up to 75 would be obtaining insurance through the exchanges rather than traditional Medicare.

On the Medicaid side, low-income beneficiaries would migrate onto the exchanges for routine medical care and have the federal government pick up the full tab. But states that accepted the federal funding would have to take over financial and administrative control of long-term care (such as nursing home stays for elderly and disabled beneficiaries).

One easy way to think about Roy's plan is that it envisions eventually moving all government-sponsored health coverage over to a version of an exchange, though the government would use a lighter regulatory hand on his brand of exchanges than the ones that exist within Obamacare.

According to estimates Roy had done on the plan, it would cut taxes and spending while insuring 12.1 million more people than Obamacare by 2025. He said the increase in coverage would mainly be due to the fact that his plan would make it cheaper and more attractive for younger Americans to buy insurance

To be clear, Roy would be reducing taxes and spending when compared to Obamacare. This is a technical point, but a significant one that is worth taking a moment to clarify, because disagreements over the best way to measure taxes and spending are one of the major dividing lines among the Obamacare alternatives we're exploring in this book.

Any policy proposal in Washington that is making its way through Congress must be evaluated over a period of time against projections of what taxes and spending would be over that same period if that proposal were never enacted. This is known as the budget baseline. Once a given proposal passes through Congress and becomes law, the baseline gets revised to reflect the new level of taxes and spending.

In the case of Obamacare, according to the Congressional Budget Office, the law will spend around $1.8 trillion[48] over the next decade on expanding insurance coverage and raise taxes by about $1 trillion.[49] Republicans voted against that

---

48   "Updated Estimates of the Effects of the Insurance Coverage Provisions of the Affordable Care Act." Congressional Budget Office. April 2014. **https://www. cbo.gov/publication/45231**

49   The CBO determined that a combination of tax increases and cuts to projected spending on Medicare would offset the costs of the coverage expansion, but it has not done a full assessment of the deficit effects of the law since 2012.

spending when Obamacare passed. But now it's part of the baseline, so they face a choice.

They could simply repeal Obamacare, wiping out all of its spending and taxation, and start building an alternative from that clean slate. But then, any money that they spend would be recorded as a spending hike. Instead, if they keep the current baseline on the books, which includes Obamacare, they can still spend a lot of money on a new plan to subsidize insurance, and as long as they spend less than $1.8 trillion, they can say that it's a spending cut.

Roy's plan keeps a good chunk of Obamacare's spending on insurance subsidies and Medicaid, but because he relies on the baseline that assumes Obamacare, he's able to claim that his plan saves $283 billion over the first decade. He argues that, like it or not, Obamacare is the baseline, so it wouldn't make sense to assume an alternate reality in which it isn't the law.

But Roy contends that looking at the first 10 years of his plan isn't the way to evaluate it, because the big savings come from its reforms to Medicare, which are only implemented gradually.

"The only way you're going to crash the spending in the first decade is if you decide you don't want to cover people and you just want to repeal Obamacare and replace it with token reforms or modest reforms," Roy said. "The first decade isn't what's important. What matters are the long-term fiscal liabilities, which are gigantic. So the goal with this plan is to make gradual adjustments that really take hold over a long period of time."

After the Medicare reforms have had time to kick in, estimates Roy had done for his plan claim it would reduce deficits by $8 trillion over 30 years, cut taxes by $2.5 trillion over the same period, and make Medicare solvent in the long-term.

Although Roy's proposal could theoretically be implemented as part of a "repeal and replace" plan, it wouldn't make much sense to do it that way. Because he preserves a number of elements of Obamacare (such as the exchanges) it would require extra effort to break everything down and rebuild it again. So it's better thought of as a comprehensive plan to reform the health care system as it exists in a post-Obamacare world.

From a philosophical standpoint, supporting Roy's proposal would be a huge leap for limited government conservatives. Not only would they be expected to embrace the goal of universal coverage, but they would have to cede major ground to Obamacare on taxes, spending, and regulations. Remember, among other things, Roy's plan keeps some of Obamacare's taxes, preserves its exchanges, maintains the requirement that insurers have to cover those with pre-existing conditions, and still provides generous subsidies.

Roy rejects the characterization of his plan as surrendering to Obamacare.

"Obamacare is the law of the land," he told me. "It has been for four years and will be at least for seven years [assuming it can't be repealed until 2017, after Obama leaves office]. So, my view has always been that we have to, on the conservative side, contend with that. I don't see that as a concession. I just see that as the real world."

Nonetheless, by leaving so much of Obamacare's central architecture in place, the plan maintains an opening for future Democratic administrations. As long as the exchanges are still in place, it wouldn't be very difficult for Democrats to restore or even expand any regulations Roy's plan undid. In addition, it would be easy for Democrats to repeal changes to Medicare and Medicaid before they have a chance to really take hold.

"You let the camel's nose under the tent…and then before you know it, then there's a new administration and things move forward and you're more on the path to a single-payer kind of system or more Obamacare," warned Sally Pipes of the Pacific Research Institute, who believes a full repeal is necessary.

Even putting aside philosophical objections and looking at it pragmatically, it isn't clear that Roy's plan would be politically palatable, even though he has described political feasibility as one of his primary reasons for choosing to design his plan the way he did. The proposal aims to attract a broad coalition of Republicans and Democrats, but many components of the plan could end up turning off both sides.

To date, Democrats have been reluctant to support any significant changes to Obamacare and have ferociously attacked the types of changes to Medicare and Medicaid being contemplated by Roy. The idea that even a handful of Senate Democrats would get behind legislation that would simultaneously (from their perspective) weaken Obamacare and destroy Medicare and Medicaid is pretty difficult to imagine.

Broadly speaking, Democrats would view it as a significant concession just to support changes to Obamacare that, among other things, would allow insurers to hike premiums on older beneficiaries. Roy's plan would ask them, on top of that, to raise the retirement age for Medicare and turn it into a more competition-based program along with Medicaid. It's worth keeping in mind that Congress has never successfully raised the retirement age of Medicare due to the fierce political backlash that occurs when politicians merely suggest it. Yet Roy's proposal for Medicare depends on members of Congress sitting back and allowing the retirement age to increase each and every year, in the face of intense lobbying.

Those who argue that there is theoretical Democratic support for a version of a Medicare reform that moved the system to one that gives seniors a choice among competing private plans often point to Sen. Ron Wyden, a liberal Democrat from Oregon, who endorsed a version of this in 2011, after negotiations with Paul Ryan. But Wyden stipulated at the time that he was only willing to endorse this brand of Medicare reform in theory based on the assumption that Obamacare remained untouched.[50]

Roy insisted that by maintaining a modified version of Obamacare's exchanges, he would be making it difficult for Democrats to demonize a plan to migrate seniors into them.

"I've tried to look and say, okay, how am I reforming entitlements?" Roy asks rhetorically, to demonstrate how he would flip the tables in a theoretical debate with Democrats. "By taking a program that you all installed, that you all have been defending, and telling me for the last seven years is the greatest thing since sliced bread, or (at least) think it's serving people very well and we should all support it, now you're turning around and saying while that program is really great for 64-year-olds, it's terrible and destructive for 65-year-olds."

But employing such an argument would require a high-wire act from Roy and anybody inclined to support his plan. On the one hand, supporters of his plan seeking Democratic buy-in would have to be arguing that it would effectively be offering Obamacare to older Americans. On the other hand, to prevent an erosion of support on the Republican side, the supporters would have to reassure conservatives that the new plan was substantially different from Obamacare.

---

50   Klein, Philip. "Ryan's bombshell Medicare compromise." *Washington Examiner.* Dec. 15, 2011. **http://www.washingtonexaminer.com/ ryans-bombshell-medicare-compromise/article/1008751**

Beyond the difficulty of convincing the various political co-alitions to get behind such a plan, there are the challenges involved in winning over the broader public. First, the plan would be lumping together reforms to a program that was passed in 2010 and that remains unpopular, with an overhaul of Medicare – a program that has broad public support and has been on the books since 1965. Second, a central popu-list criticism of Obamacare was that it was an overly complex, 2,000-page bill. Any legislation based on Roy's model would also be incredibly long and complex, potentially provoking a similar backlash.

Roy himself notes that his plan is modular, meaning that it may not be the type of proposal that passes all at once, but perhaps it's something that Republicans could pass in parts, or combine with other legislation. For instance, if Republi-cans want to repeal the individual mandate, his plan offers one possible approach to do so without causing a major dis-ruption to the insurance market.

Ultimately, how opponents of Obamacare evaluate the Re-form School depends on how much of the law they believe is in play. To those who believe that repealing Obamacare is no longer a realistic option, any effort to make it less burden-some and more market-friendly (especially when coupled with free market reforms to older entitlements), is no doubt preferable to the Obamacare status quo. But those who be-lieve repealing the law is still within reach may be more interested in another approach. So, let's see what's behind door number two...

Chapter 5
THE REPLACE SCHOOL

In March 2010, weeks before the final passage of Obamacare, then-House Speaker Nancy Pelosi declared, "We have to pass the bill so that you can find out what is in it."[51] These 16 words are among the most infamous ever uttered in connection with Obamacare, but they are also among the most misunderstood.

Most people view this statement as her suggesting that neither she nor anybody knew what was actually in the bill being voted on (which may be true, but it wasn't what she was trying to say). Pelosi added, in a less quoted phrase, "away from the fog of the controversy."

Her overarching point was one being made by supporters of the legislation from Obama on down, trying to get the bill across the Congressional finish line. The theory was that Obamacare was only unpopular because it was at the center of a yearlong bitter legislative battle in which all of the public's attention was focused on the ugly sausage-making aspects of moving a large proposal through Congress. The wishful thinking was that because the law had not been implemented, it was easily caricatured by its opponents. Pass it, Pelosi and others were arguing, and the public would realize the benefits of the law, and it would become popular.

---

51   See video: **https://www.youtube.com/watch?v=hV-05TLiiLU**

This wasn't to be. In November 2014, four and a half years after the law passed and roughly a year since its major benefits started being distributed, public approval of the law sank to a new low of 37 percent, according to Gallup, with 56 percent expressing disapproval.[52] The Kaiser Family Foundation, which has been doing a regular tracking poll[53] on the law since it passed, has similar findings. In April 2010, a 46 percent plurality of the public favored the law, compared to 40 percent who had an unfavorable view. But by November 2014, the unfavorable rating had shot up to 46 percent, while favorability sank to 37 percent. What's even more incredible is that the same poll found that among the uninsured – the segment of the population that Obamacare is most directly intended to benefit – favorability was even lower, at just 29 percent.

Keeping this in mind, there's another school of thinking on the right, the Replace School, which holds that Obamacare's persistent unpopularity means that it shouldn't be treated as being set in stone. Unlike those in the Reform School, those in the Replace School believe it can be fully repealed, but only if Republicans offer a credible alternative to the uninsured.

---

52   McCarthy, Justin. "As New Enrollment Period Starts, ACA Approval at 37%." Gallup. Nov. 17, 2014. http://www.gallup.com/poll/179426/new-enrollment-period-starts-aca-approval.aspx

53   "Health Tracking Poll: Exploring the Public's Views on the Affordable Care Act (ACA)." Kaiser Family Foundation. http://kff.org/interactive/health-tracking-poll-exploring-the-publics-views-on-the-affordable-care-act-aca/

"You're going to have to do replace with repeal," said Jim Capretta of the Ethics and Public Policy Center and American Enterprise Institute, whose work has influenced the thinking behind several Republican alternatives. "You can't displace this incumbent program without a replace program, in my judgment."

Jeff Anderson, executive director of the 2017 Project, a policy organization that has put out an Obamacare alternative of its own, said, "I think the idea that it can't be repealed is crazy. I think it's more of a question of how can Republicans possibly fail to repeal it in light of having the public on their side for more than an Olympiad."

Moreover, policy-wise, Anderson doesn't think it's possible to get to anything remotely replicating a free market health care alternative without full repeal of the existing law.

"I think it's a mistake to play too much on Obamacare's turf, and say we should be sort of like it, or keep provisions of it," he said. "I certainly don't think it's remotely fixable. I think we clearly need to wipe the 2,700 pages off the books, start from scratch, and strive for real reform that moves things in a conservative direction from the pre-Obamacare status quo."

Anderson argued that to be credible as an alternative, any replacement has to account for Obamacare's beneficiaries. "I don't think it's politically viable to say you're going to yank people back off coverage and have no answer for that," he explained.

Yuval Levin, a fellow at the Ethics and Public Policy Center and a former health care policy adviser in the Bush White House, stated things a little differently.

"I think repeal has to be connected to a replacement," Levin said. "And in that sense, the difference between repealing and replacing is a smaller difference than we sometimes think. It seems to me that understanding a better health care system as a substitute for Obamacare is important to understanding what's wrong with Obamacare."

He explained, "I think the difference between left and right on health care when you begin from the pre-Obamacare status quo is a difference of direction, not a difference of degree. That means that to get to the right place, we have to undo what Obamacare did and take steps in the opposite direction, in a market-oriented direction. That effectively means repeal. Does that mean that the first line of the bill has to say that Obamacare is repealed? I guess it doesn't have to, but the thing would be a repeal. Replacing Obamacare with a better system would mean repealing it in effect."

Levin said that it didn't make sense to set a specific numerical goal for coverage. Though it could improve the politics to have a bill that offered broad coverage, he said, ultimately increased coverage would more be a natural consequence of well-crafted legislation. "I think a functional health insurance market in America would cover more people than Obamacare, because it would make it possible for people to afford at least catastrophic coverage in much larger numbers," he argued.

Though there are a number of plans within the Replace category of plans, they share a couple of key characteristics beyond calling for the repeal of Obamacare. For one, they depend on a baseline that includes Obamacare and additionally, they rely on tax credits rather than deductions as a means of allowing people to purchase insurance.

As elaborated in the prior chapter, one of the fault lines in the debate over alternatives to Obamacare is whether to compare levels of spending in any given proposal to a world in which Obamacare exists, or to a world in which it never passed. Comparing the numbers to Obamacare budgetary levels allows a plan to appear as if it's cutting taxes and spending, even though those levels of taxes and spending are higher than they would have been if Obamacare had never passed.

Like the Reform School, the Replace School compares its spending to Obamacare.

"I think Obamacare has been on the books now for more than four years, and it's kind of funny to refer back to a prior baseline," Anderson said.

Levin elaborated, "Any proposal we have should cost as little as it possibly can and it should disrupt the economy as little as it possibly can. The question of whether we should pretend we live in a world where Obamacare never happened and compare every new idea to the pre-Obamacare baseline – Obamacare has happened and is changing the health care system. And so any reform of that system now is going to have to start from this place, which we don't like. But I don't think it's possible to ignore that and think that the public so detests Obamacare that they would like to pretend it never happened. I just don't think that's right."

He added, "We lost too many elections to be able to stop Obamacare, we didn't stop it, and now in reversing it, we have to begin from where it is and push back."

The second major characteristic of plans in the Replace School is that they rely on tax credits to provide financial assistance to individuals to help them purchase insurance. Other plans, which we will explore in the next chapter, depend on deductions.

The distinction between a tax credit plan and a plan that relies on a standard tax deduction, on the surface, seems like a rather innocuous technical matter. In reality, it is the subject of fierce debate on the right, a topic so controversial that it can quickly turn a meeting of normally mild-mannered conservative health policy wonks into a bloody scene from *Game of Thrones*.

"This line of division between deduction and credit has been a point of just intense disagreement among conservative health care people," Levin said. "I mean, I think back to a meeting in 2006 in the Bush White House where it was certainly the most intense, rambunctious meeting I've ever witnessed in government – and it was just a bunch of health care people arguing between credit and deduction."

What really makes this debate so heated is that it's a proxy for a much larger philosophical debate over how much of a role the government should be playing in expanding access to health insurance.

A tax deduction merely reduces individuals' tax liability. So, for instance, if somebody earning $50,000 receives a $10,000 deduction, that person only has to pay taxes on $40,000 worth of income. Creating a deduction for individuals to purchase insurance is a purer limited government approach, because it's effectively just a tax cut.

The drawback of such an approach for those seeking to expand coverage is that it wouldn't benefit individuals who owe little or no money in taxes against which to take advantage of the deduction, a population heavily represented among the uninsured. That's why others on the right prefer handing individuals a tax credit to purchase coverage. If a tax credit is $2,000, for instance, and an individual doesn't owe the government any taxes, that person would still receive $2,000 from the federal government.

"It doesn't make sense to me that the role of the federal government only applies to people who have an income tax liability," Levin said.

Because more people would be able to take advantage of a tax credit to shop for coverage than a deduction, Levin said, it would do more to foster a strong market for health insurance.

Anderson explained, "It comes down to, if you want to get rid of Obamacare, you have to have an answer for what you're going to have to do with the newly covered people – and a tax deduction does nothing for them. Because the deduction pretty much benefits the upper–middle class on up and people who pay little or nothing in taxes get little or nothing in the way of deduction. They're going to lose their insurance. Whereas a credit would allow these people to have something that they could use to buy insurance. So, it's the price to pay to beat back Obamacare. I think it's an extremely small price to pay. If we were operating in a complete political vacuum, I might not put forward a refundable tax credit, but we're not."

Guided by similar thinking, on Jan. 27, 2014, just a few weeks after Americans started receiving Obamacare benefits, a group of three Republican Senators (Tom Coburn, R-Okla., Richard Burr, R-N.C., and Orrin Hatch, R-Utah) came together to unveil a health care proposal named the "Patient Choice, Affordability, Responsibility, and Empowerment Act," or CARE.[54]

---

54   "Burr, Coburn, Hatch unveil Obamacare Replacement Plan." Jan. 27, 2014. http://www.coburn.senate.gov/public/index. cfm/rightnow?ContentRecord_id=7ef8f0d5-bf56-4ea3-80fe-7f86765a00ca&ContentType_id=b4672ca4-3752-49c3-bffc-fd099b51c966

The bill would fully repeal Obamacare, though it would restore some of its elements. As is the case with Obamacare, insurers would be barred from imposing lifetime limits on medical claims – meaning that people who develop major disabilities or debilitating diseases wouldn't have to worry about getting cut off from their insurance as their bills pile up. The bill would also require insurers to allow individuals to remain on their parents' policies until the age of 26.

The Coburn-Burr-Hatch proposal would create a federal benchmark allowing insurers to charge older Americans five times as much as younger Americans (as opposed to the three-to-one ratio in Obamacare). However, states would be permitted to set their own ratio below that amount, or opt out of the requirement altogether if they don't want to put a cap on how much older residents can be charged.

To address those with pre-existing conditions, the proposal would require insurers to offer coverage to anybody who has applied as long as they have maintained continuous coverage, regardless of whether they are switching health plans or shifting from employer-based health care to the individual market. The theory is that this would offer some protection to those with pre-existing conditions without having the same effect on premiums as Obamacare, which outright bans insurers from refusing coverage based on health status. At the same time, the authors expect that this would create an incentive for everybody to maintain their insurance coverage, thus negating the need for the individual mandate.

Furthermore, though the plan wouldn't get rid of the current tax-advantaged status for employer-based insurance, it would cap the amount that is exempt from taxes at 65 percent of the cost of an average plan.

The savings generated by capping the exclusion would be used to help finance tax credits to be offered to individuals earning up to 300 percent of the federal poverty level (or annual earnings of about $35,000 for an individual). A new division of the U.S. Department of Treasury known as the Office of Health Financing would administer the credits, which would also be adjusted based on age. As an example, individuals earning 200 percent of the poverty level (about $23,000) between the ages of 18 and 34 would receive a tax credit worth $1,560, while somebody of the same income level between the ages of 50 and 64 would receive $3,720. By comparison, Obamacare's subsidies can be claimed by individuals earning up to about $47,000.

In cases where individuals qualify for a tax credit high enough to cover the cost of a plan but never sign up for insurance, states have the option of automatically enrolling them in a default policy. If they don't want to be enrolled, individuals would also have the ability to opt out.

The proposal would also expand the use of tax-free health savings accounts, for instance, by allowing funds to be withdrawn to pay premiums for long-term care insurance and CO-

BRA. Under existing law, HSAs can be used to pay for direct spending on medical services, but not premiums.

Instead of expanding Medicaid, as Obamacare does, the Coburn-Burr-Hatch proposal would reform it to give more flexibility to states. As Medicaid currently stands, the federal government sends money to states and sets narrow parameters for how states can serve their low-income populations. This plan would give states more freedom to tailor the program to the characteristics of their people. It would also allow Medicaid beneficiaries the option of using their tax credit to purchase private coverage.

The proposal also encourages states to adopt medical malpractice reforms. Many free market health care analysts argue that the rise of medical malpractice lawsuits inflates medical spending in several ways. To start, due to the potential financial losses associated with lawsuits, doctors and hospitals must take out expensive medical malpractice insurance. Additionally, the fear of lawsuits can lead doctors to order a lot of tests that may not be medically necessary, just so that they can defend themselves by proving that they left no stone unturned in treating the patient. This practice is known as "defensive medicine," and a 2012 survey of physicians by Jackson Healthcare found that 75 percent of doctors said they ordered medically unnecessary tests to avoid lawsuits.[55] Reforming

---

55   "Survey Findings: Physicians on Tort Reform." Jackson Healthcare. Dec. 3, 2012. http://www.jacksonhealthcare.com/media-room/surveys/physicians-on-tort-reform/

the legal system to limit frivolous lawsuits is another idea for lowering health costs.

The plan would cover slightly more individuals than Obamacare, according to a private analysis conducted by the Center for Health and Economy, whose board includes Doug Holtz-Eakin, former Congressional Budget Office director and economic adviser on John McCain's 2008 campaign.[56]

A few weeks after the release of this proposal, Anderson's group, the 2017 Project, released a similar proposal, with some key tweaks.

Like CARE, the 2017 Project's proposal would repeal Obamacare, offer tax credits to individuals to purchase health insurance, cap the tax exemption for employer-based health insurance without eliminating it, and address health insurance coverage for those with pre-existing conditions.

Under the 2017 Project proposal, all individuals who are either uninsured or currently insured on the individual market would be offered a tax credit, ranging from $1,200 for those younger than 35 to $3,000 for those older than 50. The value of the credits would not vary by income level, and would be scheduled to increase in value by 3 percent each year. Any

---

56   "The Patient Choice, Affordability, Responsibility, and Empowerment Act." Center for Health and Economy. Jan. 30, 2014. The estimate did also provide some details about the budgetary effects, but in an interview, Holtz-Eakin said that those estimates did not account for all of the components of Obamacare, so I left them out. Feel free to read more details here: **http://healthandeconomy.org/ the-patient-choice-affordability-responsibility-and-empowerment-act/**

money not spent on premiums could be put in a health savings account.

The decision to vary premiums by age rather than income is aimed at covering a broader swath of the population for less money, because younger Americans have access to cheaper insurance, especially in a market stripped of Obamacare's regulations.

"It also means you don't need to know people's income, which makes a huge difference in administering this kind of proposal," Levin said. "You don't need to have the IRS data, you don't need to know what people make. There's a set credit, it's based on age. That makes more sense than means-testing."

To address the issue of individuals with pre-existing conditions, the plan would also require insurers to continue offering coverage to those with pre-existing conditions who are covered at the time of the enactment of the proposal, including those who obtained insurance through Obamacare.

The proposal would also increase funding for high-risk pools. This is a mechanism for taking a population of people who have chronic or pre-existing conditions out of the regular insurance market and placing them in a separate group. Once there, they can purchase coverage, and insurers who take on a disproportionate number of very sick enrollees with high medical claims can receive government-backed compensation.

In addition, the proposal would cap the employer-sponsored health insurance tax exemption. As an example, "If a family plan costs, say, $22,000 and the cap is set at $20,000, a family with that plan would continue to get a tax break on the first $20,000 of its cost; it simply wouldn't get a tax break on the last $2,000."

Anderson's plan doesn't include an overhaul to Medicare, which he argued, while an important policy goal, would be a distraction from the more pressing task.

"It's certainly going in reverse, in my mind, to say programs that have been on the books for 50 years and that have become entrenched have to be dealt with before one that is very tenuous, has only been on the books for four, and is unusually unpopular," Anderson said. "Repealing and replacing Obamacare has got to be the first priority."

A Center for Health and Economy analysis found the proposal would cover 6 million fewer individuals than Obamacare in 2023. Although it would boost the number of individuals with private insurance relative to the law, Obamacare would end up covering more individuals overall due to its expansion of Medicaid.[57]

"It's pretty clear that the solution is, repeal Obamacare, deal with the parts of the system that most needed to be reformed,

---

57 "2017 Project: 'A Winning Alternative to Obamacare.'" http://2017project. org/site/wp-content/uploads/2014/02/An-Obamacare-Alternative-Full-Proposal.pdf

namely the individual market, the people who are newly insured through Obamacare, the pre-existing conditions, and costs," Anderson said. "Deal with those in a relatively finite way as [simply] as possible... Don't bite off more than that, because that's not what the public is asking for at this point, and get that into law."

He insisted, "That would be the biggest victory in the conservative movement's history, I think you can say without really much hesitation."

Before moving on, it's worth elaborating on how the Coburn-Burr-Hatch plan and the one put out by the 2017 Project handle employer-based insurance. As explained in Chapter 3, historically, one of the main goals of free market health insurance advocates was to migrate the system away from the employer-based model into one where individuals purchased their own insurance. But both of the plans outlined above merely tinker with the system – capping, rather than moving away from – the tax-free status of employer plans.

The reluctance to scrap the employer-based system was informed by the backlash against Obama when millions of health insurance plans were cancelled as a result of the law, despite his repeated pledge that those who liked their plans could keep them. Radically changing the tax treatment of employer-based insurance, which currently enables workers to buy coverage with pre-tax income, could potentially disrupt the coverage of over 150 million Americans who receive insurance this way.[58] Also, there is a view that the popularity and broad attachment to employer-based insurance is one of the remaining bulwarks against a full single-payer system.

"Right now there's clearly not a political demand for [eliminating the employer tax advantage]," Anderson said. "That's a sort of conservative or libertarian utopia that is not popular with the people who are on employer-based coverage. So I think that going after employer-based coverage or changing the tax treatment too aggressively is a pretty sure-fire way to not get to repeal."

Similarly, Capretta insisted, "I think it's really important for a replace plan to sort of tell the public up front: 'We're not going to disrupt your employer-based system.'" Capretta recalled that in his 2008 presidential campaign, John McCain released a plan that would have done away with the tax-advantaged status of employer-based health insurance and replaced it with a system of universal credits. Then-Sen. Barack Obama attacked the plan as a massive tax hike on individuals that would also spike costs for employers. A 30-second commercial featuring a rolling ball of twine symbolizing the "unraveling" of people's health care was found to be the most aired political ad of the decade.[59]

---

58   Health Insurance Coverage of the Total Population." 2013. Kaiser Family Foundation. **http://kff.org/other/state-indicator/total-population/**

59   Sullivan, Sean. "This is the single most-aired political ad in the last 10 years." *The Washington Post.* Apr. 8, 2014. **http://www.washingtonpost.com/blogs/the-fix/wp/2014/04/08/watch-obama-hit-mccain-in-the-single-most-aired-campaign-ad-of-the-past-decade/**

"I think conservatives who are talking in those kind of terms of displacing the existing tax for employer health care with a universal credit or something, I think they're really underestimating the political resistance that can be mounted to that," Capretta said.

Another proposal worth including in the broad category of Replace plans is one unveiled by Rep. Tom Price, R-Ga., an orthopedic surgeon who succeeded Paul Ryan as chairman of the House Budget Committee.[60] He released his plan in June 2013, so some technical details could change should it be re-introduced in the new session of Congress. But Price has for years been advocating a more patient-centered approach to medicine, and will likely be an influential voice in any Republican plans to push an alternative, so it's still worth understanding his plan's conceptual framework.

Like the other plans mentioned in this chapter, Price's plan, called the "Empowering Patients First Act," would fully repeal Obamacare.

"It needs to be fully repealed, because the first step out of the gate for Obamacare is a step in the wrong direction and that is for government control over every aspect of health care, so it's hard to fix the system that they have put in place without ending that premise that government ought to be running and controlling health care," Price told me.

---

60 "H.R. 2300, Empowering Patients First Act." Section-by-Section Overview. http://tomprice.house.gov/sites/tomprice.house.gov/files/HR%202300%20 Section%20by%20Section.pdf

Like other policy voices cited in this chapter, he believes broad access to coverage is an important feature of an alternative.

"Coverage is important, and our bill, the 'Empowering Patients First Act,' we believe provides not just an incentive, but the financial feasibility for every single American to purchase the coverage that they want," he said.

He added that, "The system doesn't work if people aren't covered."

Among the differences between his plan and the others mentioned in this chapter is that it relies on a blended approach of tax deductions and credits.

Price's plan would offer Americans the option of purchasing insurance on a tax-free basis, though for those receiving employer-based coverage, they would only receive an exemption from taxes on plans up to the cost of an average-priced plan. That means that if businesses want to offer plans above that average, they'd have to pay for the excess cost with after-tax, rather than pre-tax, dollars.

For those at the lower-end of the income scale who may not have enough of a tax liability to benefit from the deduction, he would offer a credit. The credit would initially be pegged at $2,000 for individuals, $4,000 for married couples filing a joint return, and $500 for each additional dependent for a maximum possible credit of $5,000. Individuals earning up to 200 percent of the federal poverty level (about $23,000) would receive the full credit, while those between 200 percent and 300 percent of the federal poverty level (about $35,000) would receive a declining credit as they moved up the income latter. The value of the credit would be adjusted for inflation.

"Credits are a challenge for some folks on my side of the aisle, and I understand that," Price acknowledged. "But the problem I have right now is that we are imprisoned by a system that doesn't provide high-quality care for many individuals in our society, especially at the lower end of the economic spectrum, because of the rules that have been put in place by the federal government. So, if we freed up the patients to select the kind of coverage that they want, we would get a model and a system that actually worked for them and not for government."

Although Price's plan wouldn't eliminate the option of employer-based health insurance, his approach could be disruptive to it if it prompts younger workers to exit the employer market to seek cheaper insurance outside. That could encourage many businesses to drop coverage, making it especially difficult for older and sicker individuals to find affordable coverage.

He said that even if that were to happen, the proposal would have a backstop. It would also allow individuals to enroll in health plans put together by large associations such as churches, alumni groups, and trade associations. So any older American who's forced into the open market because his employer stopped offering insurance would be able to band together with others to obtain affordable coverage.

The proposal would also allow insurers to sell insurance across state lines, giving more options to consumers, and it would provide funding to states to maintain high-risk pools.

A review of the plan by Holtz-Eakin's American Action Forum found that it would increase coverage through 2025, though the increase would be 6 percent less than the increase under Obamacare.[61] Price said that every American would have access to affordable coverage under his plan if they want it. There is no individual mandate, however, so people could choose not to obtain any.

Politically, the fact that all of these plans promise full repeal could make them more attractive to elected Republicans who have pledged to wipe the law off of the books than the Reform School proposals explored in the last chapter. On the other hand, for this same reason, it would be a challenge to gain any Democratic support for such an approach. Even though the plans make an effort to provide coverage to lower-income Americans, they would still disrupt the flow of benefits as they exist under Obamacare, meaning Democrats could still cite examples of individuals whose insurance would be displaced by the overhaul, at least in the short-term. Given the

---

61   Holtz-Eakin, Douglas and Parente, Stephen. "April 2014 Update: Budgetary and Coverage Impact of the Empowering Patients First Act (H.R. 2300)" American Action Forum. http://americanactionforum.org/insights/budgetary-and-coverage-impact-of-the-empowering-patients-first-act-h.r.-230

unlikelihood of attracting Democratic support, it remains unclear how much of the proposals Republicans could enact.

It's true, there is a parliamentary maneuver known as reconciliation, which allows budget-related legislation to pass with a simple majority, rather than 60 votes. The trick then becomes what can be construed as a budget item.

Democrats did use the reconciliation procedure to help get Obamacare across the congressional finish line in 2010, but only after passing an earlier version of the bill with 60 Senate votes in 2009. The parts of the current law that directly spend money could probably be repealed this way, but onerous regulations that aren't directly related to the budget likely couldn't be.

On the other end of the spectrum, there would still be Obamacare opponents who find that the plans outlined in this chapter do not go far enough and make too many concessions to the liberal health care approach. And that brings us to door number three...

Chapter 6
THE RESTART SCHOOL

On April 2, 2014, Louisiana Gov. Bobby Jindal visited Washington and met with a group of conservative health care experts and commentators to sell an alternative to Obamacare crafted by his policy group, America Next.

A certified wonk, Jindal was appointed to run the Louisiana Department of Health and Hospitals at the ripe young age of 24. He went on to serve as executive director of the National Bipartisan Commission on the Future of Medicare and, in 2001, a few months shy of his 30th birthday, President Bush named him an assistant secretary at the federal Department of Health and Human Services. His health care policy credentials, combined with his experience as governor, make him a natural figure to influence the policy debate on the right.

On this day, with many natural allies crowding around a conference table in a downtown D.C. office, Jindal found himself under fire. Policy mavens blitzed him with questions and comments suggesting that his plan likely wouldn't cover enough Americans to be considered a politically credible response in the post-Obamacare world, in which millions were already benefitting. But Jindal had an unequivocal message, which he repeated throughout the meeting.

"I don't think conservative health care reform is about, we're going to compete with [the left] in terms of how many people we say have an [insurance] card," he said. "That's not the ultimate goal."

He later elaborated, "If we start with the premise that we've gotta give every single person a card, and that's the only way we can be successful, we're done. We've adopted their metrics of success. I think our metric of success needs to be what the president said in '08, let's drive down cost… If the metric of success is gonna be which plan can say 'we've given more people more cards,' they always win. Because they will always spend more, they will always disrupt more."

When I asked him to comment on the view that the debate over repeal had changed because of the millions receiving subsidies through Obamacare, he said, "I absolutely do not think we can give up the fight to repeal Obamacare. That's the attack from the left obviously, that once you've given stuff to folks, once you've expanded a program, you can't cut it back. If as conservatives we concede that, we're done. We're done as a country and we're done as a conservative movement."

He also put it this way: "I do think it's a mistake if we argue we can't take back what Obama has already given."

To be sure, Jindal wasn't advocating for conservatives to repeal Obamacare and do nothing. Rather, he argued that they should be making the case for an overhaul that focuses on affordability, not coverage, which he said is a more pressing concern for most voters.

Indeed, there is evidence that Americans' views on the importance of achieving universal coverage are shifting. Ever since 2000, Gallup has been asking Americans whether they thought it is "the responsibility of the federal government to make sure all Americans have health care coverage" and before the Obama administration, a majority consistently said "yes," it was a government responsibility. In 2006, 69 percent of Americans said "yes," compared to 28 percent who said "no."[62] But during Obama's presidency, the numbers started to flip, and for three years in a row, a majority felt the other way. In 2014, 52 percent of Americans said that government had no responsibility to make sure all Americans have coverage, compared to 45 percent who said it did. On a net basis, that's an overall swing from a +41 margin to a -7 margin, or 48 points.

One possible interpretation is that, in theory, Americans supported the idea of expanded coverage as long as it didn't affect their medical care, but that once they were exposed to the fact that, in practice, it meant premium increases, cancelled plans, more taxes and spending, and an erosion of choices of doctors and hospitals, they changed their mind.

---

62   Newport, Frank. "Majority Say Not Gov't Duty to Provide Healthcare for All." Gallup. Nov. 20, 2014. http://www.gallup.com/poll/179501/majority-say-not-gov-duty-provide-healthcare.aspx

"I don't think with time, this gets better," Jindal said of Obamacare. "I think with time, more and more of their broken promises are exposed."

Jindal explained, "We need to focus on real health care reform that empowers the consumer, that doesn't grow government, that puts patients back in charge and allows people to continue to get access to high quality care. I think the president made a mistake when he veered from his focus on costs and I think we can reclaim the debate, re-center the debate, re-focus the debate on providing access to high quality care, driving down the cost of health care."

Although Jindal's plan and other ideas outlined in this chapter could be described as "replace" plans (because the term is often applied generally to mean any Obamacare alternative), there is a fundamental difference that warrants putting them in a separate category from the plans outlined in the previous chapter. The term "replace" implies that a plan is being crafted as a response to Obamacare, grappling with the changes that it's made to the insurance market, being conscious of the fact that Obamacare is already dispersing insurance benefits. In contrast, the proposals explored in this chapter not only want to wipe away Obamacare, but they want to then proceed without getting hung up on the changes that the law has already made to the health care sector. The proponents of this line of thinking would essentially reform the health care system just as they would have if they'd had the chance to do so in 2009, before Obamacare passed. That's why I draw a distinction between the two approaches, and refer to the group of ideas explored in this chapter as the Restart School.

In crafting his proposal, beyond repealing Obamacare and aiming to reduce costs, Jindal decided that he wanted to make sure he didn't raise taxes or spending, not just relative to Obamacare, but relative to the pre-Obamacare world. He would get rid of all of the taxes and spending in Obamacare first, and then make sure that he didn't restore any of it. Put another way, he didn't want to use any spending or tax revenue from Obamacare to finance a conservative alternative. "I'm not spending the Obamacare money," he insisted. This is a significant departure from the plans we've looked at up through this point, though the view does have other prominent backers.

Jindal's approach on tax and spending levels was echoed by House Ways and Means Chair Rep. Paul Ryan. Ryan, who is still in discussions with other lawmakers about signing on to his own alternative, told me in a September 2014 interview that he agreed with Jindal on this point.

"I'd go back to the pre-Obamacare baseline is what I'd do," Ryan said. "I think that's the way to go, because we shouldn't assume we're going to have an explosive entitlement and then just replace it with our own. So I would go back to the pre-Obamacare – I would start over, quite frankly."

Ryan insisted, "It's a fiasco, let's call it for what it is, let's wipe the slate clean, let's start over."[63]

Once Obamacare is eliminated, Jindal's proposal would create a system that equalizes the tax treatment of health insurance. Instead of merely giving tax advantages to those who obtain insurance through their employers, the Jindal plan would create a standard deduction for health insurance for all taxpayers. The deduction could be applied against both income and payroll taxes (the 7.65 percent in taxes that nearly all Americans pay to theoretically[64] help finance Social Security and Medicare).

One question this raises is whether Jindal's proposal would be politically toxic by being too disruptive to the existing employer insurance market. As it stands now, because employers represent larger pools of people of various ages, they're able to keep costs relatively stable. Insurers don't have to jack up prices on older employees, because in a large enough company, there are still plenty of younger employees with low medical claims to balance out the costs. But if Americans were able to enjoy the same tax treatment by purchasing insurance on their own, younger and healthier workers who could easily find cheap insurance on the individual market would be more likely to seek insurance on their own. Any sort of exodus of

---

63   See video of the interview: **http://www.washingtonexaminer.com/ article/2553760**

64   Social Security and Medicare taxes are regularly used to finance other government spending.

young and healthy individuals from the employer market would mean that businesses would be stuck with the older and sicker workers, driving up the cost of offering coverage. That may cause many businesses to stop offering coverage altogether.

This is the reason why plans such as the Coburn-Burr-Hatch plan and the 2017 Project plan discussed in the previous chapter offered a tax credit only to individuals who don't have employer insurance. That way, they could only access a credit if they quit their jobs, making it much less likely that they'd jump ship.

Jindal insisted that his plan would actually be less disruptive to the employer market. He pointed out that tax credit-based plans are financed by limiting the value of employer health insurance that can be exempt from taxation. This feature, he argued, would encourage employers to drop more expensive health plans, and so it would immediately rock the employer-based insurance market.

In contrast, he argued, his proposal would start off with a deduction that would be generous enough to allow for plans that offered rich benefits, so the initial effects would be limited. Over time, the dollar value of the deduction would grow to keep up with inflation.[65] Eventually, this approach would still cause a migration away from the employer-based market,

---

65   Over time, the growth of the value of the deduction would be pegged to the Consumer Price Index, which is the standard rate of inflation. Traditionally, health care costs have grown at a faster rate than standard CPI, but Jindal argues that the

he conceded, but he said the change would only happen gradually and only after other reforms in his proposal achieved a reduction in the overall rate of growth of health costs.

His plan would expand health savings accounts to allow them to be used to pay for premiums, rather than merely direct medical expenses. He would also give insurers and employers greater ability to design plans that incentivize healthier behaviors (such as offering discounts for eating right, quitting smoking, and getting regular exercise). This, in turn, would reduce health spending in the long run by cutting down on health problems that are directly related to individual behaviors.

The proposal would also allow small businesses or individuals to gather together to form associations allowing them to purchase coverage with a broader pool. It would permit the sale of insurance across state lines, a move targeted at allowing individuals to purchase cheaper insurance free of many of the mandates proposed at the state level. It would also loosen requirements on medical licensing. Given the shortage of doctors, this would allow a broader range of trained medical professionals to deliver basic care.

Jindal's reform should not be seen as a pure free market plan. For instance, he provides for $100 billion in grant money over the course of a decade to states to help them cover low-income individuals and those with pre-existing conditions. The

---

reforms he's making will bring down health costs by the time the deduction gets pegged to CPI.

states would have flexibility over how they use the money, but they must be able to demonstrate progress providing access to these populations.

Having a solution for those with pre-existing conditions is likely to be the biggest challenge for any free market plan, because it's difficult for insurers to set premiums at a level that would make it profitable to cover individuals who have chronic conditions associated with staggering medical bills. But given the political difficulty of ignoring the plight of Americans who, through no fault of their own, are suffering from such illnesses, many conservatives have embraced ideas that would provide some sort of subsidization for this population.

The way Obamacare approached the issue is a perfect illustration of how big government begets big government. Obamacare simply requires insurers to cover those with pre-existing conditions. Doing that in isolation would have prompted insurers to simply offer insurance to sicker Americans at rates nobody could afford. So that led to another provision that prevented insurers from charging sicker people more. That, in turn, led to the individual mandate, which provided more reassurance to insurers that they'd be able to sign up enough healthier customers to offset the costs of taking on the medical costs of the very sick. But once government mandated that individuals purchase insurance, bureaucrats had to define what constituted insurance, and the Obama administration's narrow definition of insurance limited choices for all other Americans. Furthermore, once individuals were required to purchase insurance, it was only fair to provide subsidies to those who could not afford it, which required more spending, and higher levels of taxation.

So, in the name of solving the problem of insurance companies denying coverage to those with pre-existing conditions – a problem that by some estimates affected less than one percent[66] of the population – Obamacare disrupted the entire health care system.

As described in Chapter 5, high-risk pools would create a separate market for those with pre-existing conditions that would compensate insurers who take on a disproportionate number of individuals with chronic illnesses. If those with pre-existing conditions can be covered separately and removed from the broader insurance market, it would make it easier to create a functioning free market for everybody else.

"I think the President was right that there was a problem – not as big as he was saying – but there was a problem for folks with pre-existing conditions," Jindal said.

He went on to say, "I don't think the answer is to upend the entire private insurance marketplace or to have the federal government come in with a one size fits all approach. So, I think states are better positioned to do that."

---

66   Roderick Gregory, Paul. "Obama's Pre-existing Conditions Whopper." *Forbes.* Oct. 8, 2013. http://www.forbes.com/sites/paulroderickgregory/2013/10/08/lying-with-statistics-obamas-pre-existing-conditions-crisis/

He argued that his approach would be "the least intrusive, best way to legitimately help those with pre-existing conditions rather than upsetting the entire apple cart of private insurance the way the president's plan does."

The funding for his plan, he said, would be paid for many times over by other reforms he proposes, such as moving to a Paul Ryan-style model for Medicare in which seniors would receive subsidies to choose among privately-administered insurance policies, as opposed to the current system in which all seniors must enroll in a single government-run program. Instead of maintaining the current Medicaid system, in which the federal government sends money to the states with a lot of strings attached, Jindal's plan would provide annual grants to the states and allow them the flexibility to find innovative ways to deliver care to low-income Americans.

No cost estimate has been done on Jindal's plan, but he does cite an analysis done by the Lewin Group in 2007 on a proposal by President Bush that followed a similar deduction-based approach.[67] That analysis found Bush's plan would have increased the number of insured Americans by 9.2 million, which would have represented an expansion of coverage if the plan were adopted at the time. But such gains are modest compared to the 26 million people that Obamacare

---

67   Sheils, John and Haught, Randy. "President Bush's Health Care Tax Deduction Proposal: Coverage, Cost and Distributional Impacts." The Lewin Group. http://www.lewin.com/~/media/Lewin/Site_Sections/PressReleases/Bush-HealthCarePlanAnalysisRev.pdf

will add to the insurance rolls, according to the CBO.[68] The Lewin analysis also found that the Bush proposal "would disproportionately increase coverage among higher income groups."

Jindal acknowledged that other plans that spend more money could extend coverage to more people. "If you're willing to raise more taxes, you are able to give more people more stuff," he said.

But he said that, "Whatever line we draw, they're going to be willing to spend a dollar more, on everything, from college tuition, from health care, from minimum wage, from anything…The American people are smart enough to know that's not sustainable. That everything can't be free. That the government simply can't do everything for everybody. There's a cost to that. Whether it's slower economic growth, whether it's more debt, whether it's higher tax rates…The government's not making wealth. All it's doing when it's trying to redistribute is it's slowing down the growth in this country that makes all that possible in the first place… I think we're an aspirational people. I think the American people, they rightfully reject this idea, this cradle-to-grave, government's going to take care of everything."

---

68   "Insurance Coverage Provisions of the Affordable Care Act — CBO's April 2014 Baseline." Congressional Budget Office. **https://www.cbo.gov/sites/default/files/cbofiles/attachments/43900-2014-04-ACAtables2.pdf**

Jindal also grudgingly gave credit to Obama for being willing to pay a political price to advance his agenda and said Republicans needed to be willing to do the same.

"I think if you went back in time and found then-Senator Obama and said, 'You're going to be elected president, if you do Obamacare, you're going to lose the House, lose the ability to do anything else, or get any of your other big domestic policies through Congress,' I think he'd still do it," Jindal postulated.

He explained, "For them, they understand, this is a once in a generational opportunity to grow the size of government and encroach on our liberties."

He said Republicans should be thinking the same way and willing to risk political blowback to repeal Obamacare and push a market-based alternative. "But I think the way you get a majority of the American people convinced is to win that debate of ideas," he said. "It's to be specific and to be willing to look at people and say, 'We're going to do this and we're not going to do that.' And not everybody is going to agree with it. And that's okay."

The Republican Study Committee, a group comprised of House conservatives, unveiled a plan in September 2013[69] that pursued a similar approach to Jindal, called the Ameri-

---

69   "RSC unveils the American Health Reform Act." Sept. 18, 2013. http://rsc.woodall.house.gov/uploadedfiles/113_rsc_health_care_bill_release.pdf

can Health Care Reform Act.[70] It was introduced by Rep. David Roe, R-Tenn., and gained 133 co-sponsors.

After fully repealing Obamacare, the legislation would level the playing field between individuals purchasing insurance on their own and those obtaining it through their employer, providing a standard tax deduction of $7,500 for individuals and $20,000 for families, which could be applied against income and payroll taxes. Americans who bought cheaper plans would be able to keep the remaining value of the tax deduction, thus providing an incentive for them to buy prudently.

The bill would also increase annual limits for contributions into health savings accounts and allow individuals to purchase insurance across state lines.

Similar to the Jindal plan, the RSC would provide funding for state-level high-risk pools, though it would be less, at $25 billion over a decade.

It would also restore tax and spending levels to pre-Obamacare levels.

"We start by fully repealing, so we would want to start from pre-Obamacare days and build a plan completely separate as if that was never law," Tiffany McGuffee Haverly, Roe's communications director, said.

---

70   "The American Health Care Reform Act: A Better Way." http://rsc.woodall.house.gov/solutions/rsc-betterway.htm

She also conceded, "You're not going to get the same coverage levels that you get from [the Affordable Care Act][71] because of the simple fact that you're not requiring people to opt into this system."

Michael Cannon of the libertarian Cato Institute warns conservatives of trying to play too much on the liberals' turf, though he'd go about reforming the system in a different way than the other proposals outlined in this chapter.

It should be noted, to start with, that Cannon is one of the intellectual architects behind a Supreme Court challenge to the Obama administration's implementation of Obamacare that could have major consequences on health policy.

At issue in the case, *King v. Burwell,* are the subsidies that the federal government provides for individuals purchasing insurance through Obamacare. Though the text of the law says the subsidies were to go to individuals obtaining insurance through an "exchange established by a state,"[72] a rule released by the Internal Revenue Service subsequently instructed that subsidies would also apply to exchanges set up on behalf of states by the federal government.

If the Supreme Court were to invalidate the IRS ruling, it would make it illegal for the Obama administration to send subsidies to individuals in 36 states that declined to set up

---

71   The formal legislative name for Obamacare.

72   For one example of the phrase appearing in the law, see Sec. 1311, (d), (1).
https://www.govtrack.us/congress/bills/111/hr3590/text

their own exchanges and instead defaulted to the federal Healthcare.gov exchange.

This would have a number of implications. It would save taxpayers hundreds of billions of dollars in subsidies that otherwise would have gone out to individuals to purchase insurance. But, by exposing those individuals to the full sticker price of health insurance (a sticker price that was inflated by Obamacare), millions could lose their coverage.

Furthermore, it would effectively end the employer mandate in those 36 states, because Obamacare's penalties imposed on businesses that don't offer acceptable health insurance are only triggered when any of their workers seek federal subsidies. If such subsidies are declared illegal in those states, then no workers can collect them and so there are no penalties on employers for not providing insurance.

A ruling against the administration would also weaken the individual mandate, because those who cannot find insurance options deemed "affordable" (defined as coverage costing less than 8 percent of household income) are exempted from the mandate. Without the subsidies, more individuals would be able to claim this exemption.

A decision is expected by the end of June 2015, and given all of the potential ramifications, it's all the more reason for Republicans to have alternative ideas ready should the Supreme Court provide an opportunity to re-open the law.

"Conservatives are falling into the same trap now that they fell into with fighting the Clinton health plan…" Cannon argued. "And that is, they're conceding the left's premises that the government should be trying to provide everybody with health insurance, or the government should be trying to expand access to health insurance, or the government should be subsidizing health insurance, because some people need help and therefore the federal government should be the one to help them. The problem [comes] because once you accept those premises, all of your solutions look like the left's solutions. They look like Obamacare. And so a lot of conservatives, as much as they want to repeal it and say they want to repeal Obamacare, they're still pushing replace plans that amount to 'Obamacare Lite.'"

Cannon was particularly critical of tax credit plans. He argued that they are essentially Obamacare by another name. Not only do they represent government subsidies, he explained, but once the government says that individuals can receive a tax credit for purchasing health insurance, then the government has to define what counts as health insurance that would qualify people to receive credits. At the same time, those who didn't purchase insurance would be unable to claim the credit. Cannon said this ends up putting individuals in the same position as under Obamacare's individual mandate: purchase the type of insurance government deems acceptable or your tax liability will be higher.

"They need to stop thinking within a left-wing box," Cannon said. "And stop adopting left-wing premises and instead decide that what they want to do is make health care better and more affordable, and access to care more secure. And let that be their guide instead of expanding coverage."

A number of supporters of the credit approach with whom I spoke dismissed this criticism. They argued that it would be easy to define qualifying insurance very broadly to allow for a wide variety of plans. Alternately, the federal government could just let state regulators define what constitutes qualifying insurance.

Cannon said that a deduction approach would be preferable to a credit in that it wouldn't constitute direct government spending, but he still argued it would retain a feature that he finds troublesome – the government would be in the position of defining insurance for the sake of claiming the deduction.

He argued for a different type of approach aimed at putting all health care money directly in the hands of the consumer. The current employer-based system, he said, was effectively a government program. If the tax code didn't encourage businesses to offer insurance, they'd be able to pay higher salaries, and workers could do whatever they wanted with that money.

"The tax exclusion encourages workers to surrender control over that money to someone else who then buys them health insurance," he said. "So when you lose control of your money and somebody else buys you health insurance, it's a government program."

His alternative is to change the current exclusion for employer-based health insurance into an exclusion for large health savings accounts. Under the current system, HSAs face a number of limitations. HSAs can't be created by individuals who aren't already enrolled in a qualified high-deductible plan; they can't be used to pay for health insurance premiums; and the contributions are limited to $3,350 for individuals and $6,650 for families.[73]

Under Cannon's framework, employers could put, say, $10,000 in a large HSA for individuals to use as they see fit. Workers could choose to use that money to remain in their employers' health plans, they could purchase plans of their own, or they could save the money and let it roll over to the next year to pay future medical bills. Those who are self-employed could also make large HSA contributions.

"Some people will not be able to buy health insurance, obviously, under this plan," Cannon openly conceded.

However, he said the plan would still have broad benefits. He argued that it would bring down costs because it would de-regulate the insurance market and encourage hundreds of millions of individuals to spend more prudently and to negotiate for better prices.

---

73 "Internal Revenue Bulletin: 2014-20." May 12, 2014. **http://www.irs.gov/ irb/2014-20_IRB/ar07.html**

Though it wouldn't be a pure free market solution, he said he could theoretically be convinced to support some funding for high-risk pools to cover those with pre-existing conditions, preferably at the state level, if that were the political price that needed to be paid to repeal Obamacare and usher in an otherwise market-based system.

Though Cannon supports an overhaul to Medicare, he thinks that Obamacare should be addressed first.

"My sense is the iron is hot when it comes to replacing Obamacare with market-based alternatives," he said. "I don't know if it's hot for Medicare, but we should keep pushing."

He did suggest, though, that his plan could be seen as a type of Medicare reform. Because individuals would be able to build up large HSAs during their working years, they'd have more savings available to draw on during retirement for medical expenses, which would make them less dependent on the current Medicare program. At the same time, he said, if individuals got used to having more control over their health care dollars, there would be more clamoring for reforming Medicare in a way that injected market mechanisms.

Cannon acknowledged that it's traditionally proven difficult to repeal entitlement programs, but speculated that this time could be different.

"There is a time tested political law that, once you create a subsidy, it's extremely hard to make it go away, because you're going to have people depending on it who will want it preserved, which is why no one's talking about repealing Medicare, no one's talking about repealing Medicaid, or Social Security, or so on," he said. "But, none of those things are as unpopular as Obamacare is."

Over time, Americans' animosity toward the law keeps being reinforced by events, he said, such as the disclosure by Obamacare architect Jonathan Gruber that the law's authors were able to exploit "the stupidity of the American voter"[74] to get the law passed.

"If ever Congress [would be] able to take away someone's health insurance subsidies, Obamacare would be it," Cannon said.

The group of proposals explored in this chapter would require less spending and lower taxes than those detailed in earlier chapters and take a purer market-based approach. That would be their appeal to those on the right.

At the same time, though there are no doubt victims of Obamacare, there are also beneficiaries, and the media would do everything it could to amplify those voices in the face of a genuine repeal threat. This would make it especially difficult to wrangle up enough votes to get a solid free market alternative through Congress, even if it were done with a simple majority in the Senate.

---

74 See video: https://www.youtube.com/watch?v=G790p0LcgbI

For instance, listening to Jindal talk about how Republicans shouldn't get into a debate with Democrats over how many "cards" they can hand out, it was easy to imagine an ad featuring Obamacare beneficiaries saying that a "card" is what allowed them to be able to afford kidney dialysis, or surgery, or a host of other medical services.

It's also worth noting that at the same time there would be populist pressure against such changes, these plans would also likely be under assault by large business lobbies that now have an interest in the status quo – from insurers who would be giving up a law in which the government mandates that everybody buys their products while subsidizing them to do so, to hospitals and drug makers that benefit from millions of subsidized customers.

Ultimately, anybody inclined to embrace this approach should be prepared, in no uncertain terms, to defend themselves against ferocious attacks from the left highlighting the plight of those who would stand to lose coverage and those whom they'd argue would fall through the cracks. Supporters would have to be prepared to go on offense, outlining how such proposals could offer more freedom, lower costs, and better quality care.

Chapter 7
OVERCOMING OBAMACARE

Opponents of President Obama's health care law who have read up until this point have hopefully come away with a better understanding of the options for overcoming Obamacare. Any effort to do so will only become possible if those who don't like the law rally around an alternative approach.

As the previous chapters explored, ultimately, any approach is going to have to start with a calculus that balances principles and practical politics. People may disagree on certain principles (for instance, the importance of expanding coverage) or on the politics (whether full repeal is politically feasible, for example). They also may disagree on how much weight should be given to principles compared with political considerations. But every approach engages in this balancing act in some way. Even the most pure free market plans we explored, given political reality, are open to providing funds for some sort of government subsidies for individuals with pre-existing conditions.

Only after this more fundamental calculation is made do the technical policy details follow: whether to pursue full repeal; whether to use a credit or tax deduction; which baseline to use; and so on.

Let's recall how Obamacare passed in the first place. A single-payer health care system was the liberal ideal, but Democrats made a political calculation that it would be too disruptive and politically impossible to pursue such an approach. Barring single-payer, they wanted an optional government-run plan. But they couldn't get enough votes in the U.S. Senate to pass that. So they ended up settling for Obamacare because, even though the law enabled trillions of dollars to flow through private insurers, it still achieved many goals that were important to the left, particularly expanding insurance coverage.

At the same time, however, it should be noted that Democratic leaders dismissed warnings about the political fallout of ramming through Obamacare on a party line vote. That is, they were conscious of political reality, but ultimately, were willing to risk losing a lot of Congressional seats to advance something that was philosophically important to them.

"All these alternatives, I don't look at them as contrasting against each other, but contrasting against what we have today," said Heritage health policy analyst Nina Owcharenko. She said that sometimes the technical disagreements can obscure the areas of agreement on the right.

Most people on the right agree in broad terms about moving away from a government dominated health care system toward one that is more market oriented. The disagreement often arises over how far Republicans can go and what features are needed to really create a free market.

"I think the definition of a conservative is you get as close to free market as you can," said Tevi Troy, president of the American Health Policy Institute and a deputy secretary of Health and Human Services under President Bush.

He said Republicans have to push as far as they can within the confines of political reality, because should the party gain more power and do nothing, it only benefits the left.

"That's the way our system works," Troy said. "Each side gets their crack at the apple. Democrats took advantage of their crack at the apple in 2010 with the passage of the ACA. And so if there's still dissatisfaction with Obamacare and Republicans don't do anything about it, when Democrats get another crack at the apple, they're going more toward the direction [of more government]."

Republican control of the Senate and a spirited GOP presidential nomination contest should provide a great opportunity to debate many of the ideas explored in this book.

Those who aren't happy about the direction of American health care need to start the process of coalescing around an alternative approach. If they can do that, there's a chance to overcome Obamacare and move toward a health care system that puts the consumer first.

Acknowledgments

There are a lot of people who helped make this book a reality. First and foremost, I'd like to thank my loving wife, who was supportive and encouraging throughout the process. Despite juggling a Ph.D. dissertation and a full-time job, she spent countless hours going through various drafts of the book to help make sure I was writing in plain English rather than health care policy jargon.

I also want to thank all those who agreed to speak to me about health care policy and who helped give me access to many of the elected Republicans quoted here. Specifically, in no particular order, I'd like to thank: Grace-Marie Turner, Avik Roy, Sally Pipes, Tevi Troy, Doug Holtz-Eakin, Jeff Anderson, Jim Capretta, Yuval Levin, Nina Owcharenko, Michael Cannon, Tiffany McGuffee Haverly in Rep. David Roe's office, Rep. Tom Price and his team, Rep. Paul Ryan and his staff, Gov. Bobby Jindal and his staff, and outgoing Sen. Tom Coburn's policy team. This book was also informed by many informal and off-the-record conversations. I won't publicly name you, but you know who you are.

This book would not have been possible were it not for the efforts of a great team at the *Washington Examiner* and MediaDC. I specifically want to thank Steve Sparks, Cristina Giroux, Grace Terzian, Alex Rosenwald, Catherine Lowe, Joana Suleiman, and Chris Henderson (for the great cover illustration). I also want to thank Allen Zuk, who handled the layout and formatting.

Also instrumental were the editors I've had over the years. In an era of click-bait driven journalism, Wlady Pleszczynski of the *American Spectator,* and my editors at the *Washington Examiner* – first Stephen Smith and Mark Tapscott, and now Hugo Gurdon – have given me the time and space to write in depth about health care policy.

About the Author

Philip Klein is commentary editor of the *Washington Examiner*, where he writes about domestic politics and policy and runs the opinion section. He has emerged as one of the leading voices on health care policy on the right. His work has been cited by a diverse spectrum of media outlets, from syndicated talk radio hosts Mark Levin and Rush Limbaugh to publications including the *Wall Street Journal*, the *New York Times*, and the *Washington Post*, among many others. He formerly served as Washington correspondent for the *American Spectator* and a financial reporter for Reuters news service. He is a graduate of George Washington University, where he earned degrees in history and economics, and also holds a master's degree in journalism from Columbia University. He is the author of *Conservative Survival in the Romney Era*.

CPSIA information can be obtained at www.ICGtesting.com
Printed in the USA
LVOW06s1458060815

449113LV00019B/759/P